THE flying brownie

THE flying BROWNIE

100 Recipes for Homemade Treats That Pack Easily, Ship Fresh, and Taste Great

Shirley Fan

The Harvard Common Press
Boston, Massachusetts

The Harvard Common Press
www.harvardcommonpress.com

Printed in China
Printed on acid-free paper

Library of Congress Cataloging-in-Publication Data
Fan, Shirley.
   The flying brownie : 100 recipes for homemade treats that pack easily,
ship fresh, and taste great / Shirley Fan.
      pages cm
   Includes index.
   ISBN 978-1-55832-803-7
1. Baking. 2. Gifts. 3. Food--Packing. 4. Cookbooks. lcgft I. Title.
   TX765.F26 2013
   641.7'1--dc23
                           2012035546

Special bulk-order discounts are available on this and other Harvard
Common Press books. Companies and organizations may purchase books
for premiums or resale, or may arrange a custom edition, by contacting
the Marketing Director at the address above.

Book design by Jenny Beal Davis
Front cover photography by Joyce Oudkerk Pool; styling by Fanny Pan
Back cover and text photography and styling by Shaina Olmanson
Author photograph by Chad Borkenhagen

10 9 8 7 6 5 4 3 2 1

To my little Nils:
May you have
many delicious days
ahead.

CONTENTS

INTRODUCTION

When I was a junior in college, the peach tree in my parents' backyard flourished, producing a bounty of baseball-size fruit. Excited by their harvest, they shipped me a box of the fuzzy fruit. I checked my mailbox every day, but while other students in the university mailroom ripped open their care packages and devoured treats, those peaches never came. To this day, I still wonder what happened to that box.

Care packages are equal parts baking and arts and crafts. Not only do they bring scrumptious goodies from faraway places, they also bring cheer, love, and creativity to doorsteps around the world. Whether packed with homemade snickerdoodle cookies, cans of Hershey's chocolate syrup, or even rolls of toilet paper, care packages have a way of conveying love and eliciting feelings of comfort and care—and maybe a phone call to the dear sender!

In today's mobile world, care packages aren't just limited to students. We all know someone—whether a relative or a friend—who lives far away. If not a significant other stationed in the Middle East, a child at sleep-away camp, or a student in college, it's a sibling working abroad, an elderly aunt living across the country, or just an old friend who lives several states

away. So, while the idea of care packages may seem limited to just a small segment of the population, they're really applicable to all of us and our dispersed network of loved ones!

Throwing together a care package doesn't necessarily guarantee success, as I know firsthand. Crumbly, stale cookies or rock-hard brownies can bring down any package, no matter if the recipes belonged to Grandma or Julia Child. And poorly chosen food (fresh peaches, anyone?), flimsy boxes, careless packing, or even the wrong tape can spoil the most well-intentioned gifts. With so many potential pitfalls, assembling the perfect care package takes, well, *care*.

After years of building care packages for friends and family, I realized that there were no comprehensive practical guides or resources for putting them together. When it came to figuring out how to package and ship a batch of holiday cookies or a loaf of pumpkin bread, I had to scour the Internet and cookbooks, observe the methods that online and mail-order food companies employed, or learn through trial and error.

That's how this book came to be. Based on my notes, observations, and experiences, it's a compilation of shipping and packing tips, advice for novices and experts, and a fresh batch of thoroughly road-tested recipes. It's my hope that this book will inspire people to be creative, bake more, and send their love through thoughtfully crafted packages.

The first chapter covers the care package basics, including the best treats for shipping, how to pack and send, what materials to use, and the ins and outs of sending packages to loved ones in the Armed Forces. The following chapters feature a collection of my favorite shipping-friendly recipes that include something for everyone, from traditional Butterscotch Blondies to elegant Green Tea Shortbread Bites, from savory snacks like Sriracha Party Nuts and Everything Crackers to healthier treats such as Crunchy Spiced Apple Crisps. Each recipe has been tested for durability, lifespan, portability, and—most important—flavor.

Throughout each chapter, I've also included tips, stories, and background information to help with the baking, packing, and storing processes. Finally, the Resource Guide at the back of the book includes a list of my favorite vendors for sources related to baking, packing, and shipping the perfect care package.

Putting together a care package isn't difficult, but to send something memorable and exciting takes forethought and planning. With *The Flying Brownie*, I hope you'll find the best care package ideas, recipes, and tips to help you put together the best box you've ever made. So let's get shipping!

ACKNOWLEDGMENTS

This book started with a small idea dreamed up in a coffee shop and evolved through many months of brainstorming, writing, tasting, editing, and tasting again. It could not have been possible without the support and encouragement of many people, to whom I'm eternally grateful.

First, I am indebted to my parents for instilling in me their love and curiosity of food, and for letting me develop my baking skills at an age when I really should have been doing homework!

Thanks to Linda, Matt, Naomi, Eli, and Shaina for letting me raid your kitchen during my trips to the city and for always being my gastronomic guinea pigs. Much appreciation goes to Barb and Dick for their endless encouragement and detailed recipes, and to Ryan, Leslie, and Carter for testing and tasting recipes with great enthusiasm.

For their tireless tasting and feedback, a huge shout out to the *American Journal of Sociology* manuscript board. Glad you came to every meeting hungry! Many thanks to my other tasters: Rick, Laurie, Jan, Thomas, Eva, Melanie (and her lab), Eric, Jean, June, Erika, Sarah, and Gail.

Gracious thanks to Beth and Vallory at Wilton Industries for their support, Christianna Reinhardt for letting me pick her brain, and Jennifer Griffin at MBG Literary Management for all of her great ideas.

I am especially grateful for the guidance and mentorship of my agent, Sharon Bowers. Without her encouragement and advice, this book could not have been possible. Thank you for believing in me!

Thanks to the team at The Harvard Common Press—Dan Rosenberg, Virginia Downes, and Pat Jalbert-Levine—for taking a chance on my idea and running with it. Special thanks to Valerie Cimino and Karen Wise for their detailed editing and Shaina Olmanson and Joyce Oudkerk Pool for their beautiful photography.

To my husband, Chad, who supported and encouraged me throughout this whole project, you are incredible and I couldn't have asked for a better partner in life. Thank you for tasting everything, humoring me, and, most importantly, having the patience of Gandhi.

And last but not least, a big hug to my son, Nils, who arrived during the writing of this book. May you grow up to enjoy the sweet, the savory, and everything in between.

THE
flying brownie

CARE PACKAGES 101

A BRIEF HISTORY OF THE CARE PACKAGE

While the concept of care packages may have existed for much longer, the term *care package* has been around for less than 100 years. The name originated with the creation of the Cooperative for American Remittances to Europe (CARE) at the end of World War II. Now one of the largest humanitarian organizations in the world, CARE began with a single mission: to send life-saving provisions to survivors of the war. These "CARE Packages" were actually unused food parcels for soldiers, repurposed to benefit citizens of war-torn Europe. The first shipment of CARE Packages was delivered to residents of Le Havre, France, in 1946.

Eventually, the soldiers' leftover provisions ran out and CARE began to assemble its own parcels using donations from private companies. In the 1950s and 1960s, the packages began to include other items, such as books and clothing. CARE eventually suspended shipments to "recovered" areas in Europe and began sending packages to Asia and Latin America. CARE's shipping operation went on hiatus in the late 1960s as the organization focused on other humanitarian efforts. From 1990 to 1994, CARE briefly shipped boxes to republics of the former Soviet Union and Bosnia. Currently, CARE has resumed shipments all over the world as part of a special program to help empower women and girls.

While the CARE mission has sent 100 million packages all over the world, the impact of CARE has had a lasting effect on us. In addition to giving us the name for our special parcels, it's also inspired many of us to send comfort to people both nearby and around the world.

The first CARE Package contained items such as liver loaf, SPAM, lard, powdered eggs, and milk powder. Perhaps these don't seem like the best items to show our love and support these days, but back then they were quite literally lifesavers for many. Today's homemade care packages are often still chock full of calories, but they are mostly in the form of cakes, cookies, brownies, and the like. They bring cheer and joy to troops stationed abroad, college students pulling all-nighters, relatives recovering from illness, and faraway friends who may need a little pick-me-up for one reason or another.

PACKING UP CARE PACKAGES

Every day as I exit and enter my apartment building, I pass by a table in the lobby filled with local flyers, newsletters, and boxes. Most of the packages are in great shape, but every now and then there's a battered box that looks like it's being held together by little more than frayed packing tape and a prayer. Properly packing and shipping boxes is an important consideration when it comes to care packages. Knowing the do's and don'ts will ensure that the goodies you spent so much time creating and putting together will arrive intact for your loved

one. Let's start from the inside and work our way out.

THE GOODS

The most important part of any care package is what's inside. While it would be nice to be able to send whatever you like, care packages require treats that are able to withstand the rigors of shipping and that can stay fresh for days without refrigeration. The recipes in this book are a great start, but here are some general rules to follow for what kind of foods to pack.

- Consider sweets that are firm, dense, and/or moist, such as the Malted Chocolate Chip Cookies (page 55) or Autumn-Spiced Pumpkin Loaf (page 116). These foods are more likely to survive rough and bumpy roads and remain tasty for days. Drop cookies (chocolate chip and oatmeal), icebox/refrigerator cookies, biscotti, bars, and brownies work well. Certain softer treats, such as loaf cakes, quick breads, and muffins, also hold up well because they can absorb some shock without falling apart. Delicate, thin sweets don't fare well because they can easily crumble or fall apart.

- Firm and dry (but not brittle) savory foods such as crackers, popcorn, pretzels, and jerky ship well. Some examples from this book include the Black Pepper and Rosemary Crackers (page 133) and the Oven-Roasted Spiced Chickpeas (page 142), which are delicious and durable and have long shelf lives.

- Mixes and blends such as nuts, granola, muesli, and dried fruit keep for a long time and can even serve as insulation in care packages! Try the Sriracha Party Nuts (page 136) or the Antioxidant Berry-Nut Mix (page 150) the next time you need to fill space in a package.

- Nonfragile candies such as caramels, nougats, toffee brittle, and marshmallows are good choices. For example, the Cinnamon Marshmallows (page 102) have a forgiving texture fit for shipping, and the Chewy Mocha Caramels (page 86) are firm and dense. Be extra careful with chocolates, as they do not handle temperature fluctuations well. This can be problematic during extreme weather or when you are shipping to warm (and even cold) climates. In my recipes that use chocolate as a coating, I instruct you to temper it first to make it more durable.

Other Considerations

- Think of foods that you do not need to refrigerate and that you could leave on your counter at home for at least 5 days. If it doesn't spoil during that time period, then it will probably work in a care package. If the package is going overseas, you need to select treats that last a little bit longer. In the headnote of each recipe, I indicate how long the treat will stay fresh.

- Select foods that can withstand movement. If something can be transported and jostled a bit without crumbling or breaking, then it can most likely be shipped successfully.

- Bake small- to medium-size cookies that are at least ¼ inch thick. These will survive rough handling better than large, thin cookies.

- Items made with fresh meats and fruits are not good candidates for shipping unless you have a vacuum sealer, access to dry ice and ice packs, or boxes and insulation made especially for fresh items. Additionally, you often cannot send such goods abroad due to customs restrictions.

- If you are sending more than one item, pack each type of treat in its own airtight container or packaging. This will help keep moisture content consistent and prevent the mingling of flavors.

THE SCOOP ON INGREDIENTS

Many of the recipes in this book can be modified with different mix-ins or other flavorings. Keep in mind that some ingredients work better than others. Avoid using those that require refrigeration, such as cream cheese, whipped cream, and custard. However, on the flip side, there are also ingredients that can help extend the shelf life of baked goods, such as vegetable shortening, alcohol, honey, and raisins. Because I don't care for the taste or texture of vegetable shortening in my sweets, I use it sparingly in my own recipes. In the course of writing the book, I found a good balance between shortening and butter to create recipes that last for at least 5 days without compromising taste. I realize, though, that shortening will extend the shelf life of a treat considerably if substituted for butter. If you choose to use shortening, feel free to modify the recipes to your liking, but be sure to check the manufacturer's conversions before substituting.

FUN STUFF! FOOD SAFETY AND SPOILAGE

It's important to be extra cautious when shipping anything perishable. How long something keeps depends on a number of factors, including the type of food, the length of time the food has been unrefrigerated, how it was handled, the type of packaging, and, most important, the storage temperature.

Since spoilage is of course inevitable, as a general rule you should ship your care packages as soon as you can, using the fastest shipment method possible. Food starts aging the second it is created. I suggest that you prep baking materials the night before and bake in the morning. This ensures that you'll have sufficient time to bake, cool, wrap, and send everything by the end of the day. Planning ahead will also help you identify missing ingredients and locate boxes and mailing materials. Be sure to cool your baked goods thoroughly before wrapping them. This limits the growth of mold, which thrives in high-moisture environments.

Alternatively, you can bake ahead of time and freeze your items. Cookies and brownies can keep for up to 6 months in the freezer, while cakes and quick breads can keep for about 3 months. Make sure you freeze these baked items in zipper-top plastic bags or other airtight containers to prevent the formation of ice crystals and the absorption of unwanted freezer flavors. And be sure you thaw them before shipping them, to prevent condensation from forming inside your care package during shipping.

Last but not least, do not ship anything that you think is questionable. Use your common sense. As a former culinary school instructor warned us in class, "If in doubt, throw it out."

WE'VE GOT YOU COVERED: DRESSING AND ACCESSORIZING YOUR FOOD

Air exposure and time are your two worst enemies when it comes to keeping baked goods fresh in shipment. While we have little control over time (except for choosing the speediest shipment), we can try to minimize exposure to air. I have experimented with numerous methods of wrapping and packaging the various treats. Some of the most helpful items I used are:

Waxed paper: This can be used for wrapping treats, separating cookies in tins, or as insulation in containers.

Plastic wrap: This can be used for wrapping treats. Look for a variety of colors.

Parchment paper: Parchment is similar to waxed paper in its uses except that it can also be used in baking.

Cellophane bags and sheets: These are great for packing treats. Look for them at craft stores or in online catalogs.

Zipper-top plastic bags and airtight plastic containers: You have many choices for purchasing these inexpensive and convenient items at grocery and housewares stores. Alternatively, use sturdy pint- or quart-size take-out containers.

Food-safe metal tins with tight-fitting lids: These can be a great alternative to airtight plastic containers because they look more decorative and elegant. The downside is that they can add to the weight of a package and may also be less airtight than, say, Tupperware containers. You can purchase them at storage or housewares stores, or simply reuse cookie tins.

Cellophane tape: This type of tape is good for securing parchment, waxed paper, and cellophane around brownies or bar cookies. This creates a "finished" or professional look and makes more of a seal around the treats so they stay fresher. For packages intended for children, fun and colorful stickers could be substituted for tape.

Wrapping Basics for Your Baked Gifts

Cookies: Store in zipper-top plastic bags or airtight containers. If using plastic bags, pack them fairly full and press the air out of them so the cookies don't have room to shift around. For containers, separate the layers with parchment or waxed paper and fill empty spaces with crumpled paper.

Brownies and bars: Use plastic wrap, cellophane, or parchment or waxed paper to individually wrap the treats, secure with cellophane tape, and then store in zipper-top plastic bags. As with cookies, you may also pack unwrapped brownies or bars in tins or airtight plastic containers separated by layers of parchment or waxed paper.

Quick breads, cakes, and muffins: Wrap loaves or pieces tightly with plastic wrap (two or three layers to be sure) and then place in a zipper-top plastic bag.

Candies: Wrap each candy individually with candy foil papers, parchment paper, or waxed paper, or place candies into paper candy cups. Pack in airtight containers.

Savories: Pack crackers and snack mixes in zipper-top plastic bags so they won't be affected by moisture. Press out most of the air when sealing the bags.

Adding Extra Oomph to Your Goodies

- Bake your breads, cakes, brownies, and muffins in oven-safe disposable paper bakeware. These disposable pans do not require greasing, can withstand high temperatures, and look professional. You can also utilize disposable metal pans, but they may not look as rustic or appealing as paper bakeware. If using disposable pans, whether paper or metal, wrap treats still in the pan in clear cellophane bags and secure with string or a ribbon. This will give them a store-bought look.

- Take advantage of seasonal containers, wrapping materials, gift tags, papers, and ribbons. They can make boxes look more festive and timely, especially for the holidays. Stock up on materials after the holidays, when you can buy them at deep discounts.

- Use unexpected containers such as Mason jars, coffee cans, candy tins, and take-out boxes. For example, a great way to pack seasoned or flavored nuts is to put them in Mason jars. To decorate the jars, trace and cut out the outline of the lid on decorative paper and attach to the top of the lid with double-sided tape. Seal the jar. Make a label with the same decorative paper and then punch a hole through it. Write a message or the name of the recipe on the label and then thread it through some twine or ribbon. Tie the twine around the jar.

- Make a tall stack of cookies and brownies and pack them in cellophane bags; tie bags closed with kitchen twine, raffia ribbon, or cloth ribbon. Attach labels as above, if desired.

- Line a shallow tin with mini cupcake liners or candy paper cups and place small treats in each cup. Fill empty spaces with crumpled parchment or waxed paper to protect the candy. I like to do this with the Peppermint Fantasy

Fudge (page 88) and the No-Bake Swedish Coco Balls (page 103).

- Use stickers to decorate or seal packages. These can reflect your own personality or be geared toward the receiver. My niece is crazy about the cartoon character Dora the Explorer, so I always keep a few stickers on hand for the next time I make her something special.

NOTES AND CARDS

A note or a card within the box will help set the tone for the care package. Whether you're celebrating a birthday, sending get-well wishes, or just saying hello, it helps to send a few words so they know you are thinking of them. This can also serve as an opportunity to let the recipient know what treats are enclosed and how to store or handle them, or to share a story behind the recipe. For children, even sharing a new joke might bring a smile to their faces. Whether your card is store-bought or handmade, a personalized note is a great way to add a little extra care to your package.

PACKING SUPPLIES AND MATERIALS

Now that you know what works best inside a care package, here's what to do on the outside to make sure your gift ends its journey in the same condition as when it began traveling.

Boxes

It's very important to ship your care packages in corrugated cardboard boxes. These boxes are made from two flat pieces of cardboard that are attached by parallel grooves. This design provides heft and structure and helps guard against breakage inside the box. Corrugated boxes are manufactured to withstand specific weights, with heavier ones built for heavier things. Some boxes show their weight limit on the Box Maker's Certificate, located on one of the outside bottom flaps. There are several characteristics noted there, but pay attention to the Gross Weight Limit. Office supply stores sell corrugated cardboard boxes in various shapes and sizes; check out the Resource Guide (page 169) for some suggested vendors.

It's best to use a brand-new box when shipping because it will be sturdier, but you can also use boxes that have been previously mailed as long as they are still firm and rigid. After a few mailings, boxes tend to lose some of their strength, so be sure to examine your box for signs of tear and "softness." Remove all the tape, stickers, and labels on the outside of the box before use. Do not use a box with lots of writing all over it, since this may be confusing for the shipper and cause delays in delivery.

Tape

To securely seal a box, choose a strong tape, such as plastic packaging tape, nylon-reinforced filament tape, or water-activated reinforced tape. Use tape that is at least 2 inches wide to seal all the closures and seams of the box. You may also want to reinforce the edges of the boxes with tape to protect it further from bending. Avoid using masking tape, cellophane tape, or duct tape. These tapes are not strong enough for shipping.

Cushioning

- It's important to leave enough space in every box for cushioning. Pack according to the "4-foot-drop rule," which assumes that the contents of a box should be able to survive a 4-foot drop without damage. To do that, most shipping vendors suggest that you provide at least 2 inches of cushioning around each item and at least 2 inches of cushioning from the wall of the box. This space ensures that items will not damage each other and that the cushioning will absorb any shocks or vibrations during the shipping process.

- Many office supply stores, carrier shipping stores, hardware stores, drugstores, and housewares stores offer various types of cushioning, such as crinkle paper in various colors, Styrofoam or biodegradable peanuts, and bubble wrap, all of which can be reused. You can also use crumpled newspapers or soft things such as socks and other articles of clothing. Avoid using actual popcorn for shipping—it may be environmentally friendly, but it can also attract insects and other pests. Note that Styrofoam peanuts are not recommended for shipping to military personnel based overseas because of static cling.

Here are some general packing tips:

- Select a box that's big enough to allow extra room for cushioning.

- Put heavier items on the bottom and lighter ones on top.

- Do not under- or overstuff the box.

- Shake the box down when everything is packed to simulate shifting during shipping. If there's extra space, add more insulation.

- If you are not shipping with a vendor that uses its own specific shipping labels, use a black permanent marker to write the address in legible handwriting, and make it large enough to be read from an arm's length away. Or, even better, print out your own label and tape it onto the box. It's always easier to read something typed than something handwritten. Be sure to include your return address.

- Make sure that both addresses are complete and correct, and avoid using punctuation like commas and periods—this will help speed the package through automated processing equipment. The destination address and the return address should appear on the same side of the box, with the latter in the upper left-hand corner.

- Unless the shipper specifies otherwise, cover address labels with clear packing tape so they do not get removed or smudged.

- Label the box "FRAGILE" and "PERISHABLE."

- Do not wrap the box in paper. Some vendors have restrictions about this and will not accept a box that's wrapped.

- Do not tie the outside of the box with string, as it can get caught in sorting machinery.

SHIPPING: BY LAND, AIR, OR SEA

Of the shipping services in the United States, the three main vendors are the United States Postal Service (USPS), FedEx, and United Parcel Service (UPS). Each of the vendors offers its own unique services that are useful for shipping care packages. Numerous other businesses offer shipping services, but they may be harder to locate or less universally convenient. Feel free to use whatever shipping services you feel most comfortable with and that work best for your situation and needs.

UNITED STATES POSTAL SERVICE

As you probably know, the USPS is run by the federal government. It delivers letters and packages domestically and internationally, sells stamps, and issues money orders, among some of its many functions. While there are a number of different options for shipping care packages, Priority Mail is favored by many because of its flat-rate option and reasonable shipping times. The USPS offers free Priority Mail flat-rate boxes in various sizes with assigned rates to ship anywhere in the country. Their motto is "If it fits, it ships" (up to 70 pounds), so you pay the same rate no matter how heavy the box is. A package sent via Priority Mail generally takes 2 to 3 days to arrive, but it's not guaranteed and may get delayed due to weather or unexpected conditions. You can also use Priority Mail with your own box, though the flat rate will not apply. For faster shipping, the USPS offers Express Mail overnight service, which is guaranteed for most locations, though it is substantially more expensive than Priority Mail. Another advantage of Express Mail is that it can be delivered on Sundays and holidays for an additional fee.

Tracking and confirming the delivery of packages is generally another fee you will have to pay for at the USPS. The main advantages of using the USPS are that they offer a flat-rate service, have relatively inexpensive rates compared to other vendors, can deliver to P.O. boxes, and have a partnership with the U.S. Department of Defense, making military shipments easier (see page 24). In recent years, they've also stepped up their online services so you can create shipping labels, order stamps and materials, and schedule package pick-ups. For more, check out their website at www.usps.com.

FEDEX

Considered a premium service, FedEx is a private shipping company that offers guaranteed on-time delivery (domestic and international) and packing supplies and services. They have many storefronts and have also partnered with some office-supply and business-services chains to provide in-store service, making access easy and convenient. For packages less than 150 pounds, they offer same-day, overnight, or 2- to 3-day delivery by air, as well as ground delivery (which varies according to distance and location). They also have premium add-ons such as temperature control and "white glove"

services with specially trained drivers to ensure that packages are handled with special care.

Unlike the USPS, FedEx delivers 7 days a week, with Sunday delivery limited to certain locations in the United States. They also track all of their letters and packages and guarantee delivery. The major downside to using their services is that their rates can be quite high.

To create your own account, estimate shipping costs, create labels, track packages, or find out more about their services, go to www.fedex.com or call 1-800-GO-FEDEX (1-800-463-3339).

UNITED PARCEL SERVICE

For shipping packages, UPS seems to be the top choice for many, possibly because of the combination of their reliability, tracking services, and rates that generally fall in between those of FedEx and the USPS. Like FedEx, UPS is a private company that offers shipping and packing and guarantees their services. They also offer many shipping options, including overnight delivery and 2- to 3-day delivery via air, as well as ground delivery. They also offer value-added services such as holding for pickup, Saturday pickup, and verbal confirmation of delivery.

UPS allows you to create an online account where you can calculate shipping costs, print labels, and schedule pick-ups. You can also check out their online transit calculator to monitor where your package is. For more information, call 1-800-PICK-UPS (1-800-742-5877) or visit www.ups.com.

OTHER METHODS OF SHIPPING

Until a few years ago, DHL Express shipped both domestically and internationally, but as of this writing, you can use their services only for shipping out of the country. While their services are similar to FedEx and UPS, their ground hubs are harder to find these days. There are, however, some shipping facilities, drop boxes, and online services that enable you to print labels, schedule pickups, and order supplies. For more information, check their website, www.dhl-usa.com.

It may also be more convenient to use independent business service centers. These places offer pack and ship, office, and postal services. Though they may charge a small additional premium, they often do not have long lines or waits. Many office chain stores offer similar services, so it's worth checking with those stores if you live close to them.

INTERNATIONAL SHIPPING: GOING AROUND THE GLOBE

Shipping to the military abroad comes with its own special set of requirements; see page 24 for a discussion of shipping to overseas military personnel.

Depending on your carrier, you'll probably have to fill out some extra paperwork when sending a care package abroad. Most of the paperwork involves filling out customs forms to declare what is inside the package. Before you do that, you'll need to check on country-specific restrictions for shipping packages, since you don't want to take the time to pack a box carefully only to find out that you can't ship something that's in it. It's not uncommon for countries to have restrictions on certain edibles. (For example, it's prohibited to send the alcoholic beverage absinthe to Germany or nutmeg and vanilla to Italy.) The USPS has an extensive list of individual countries' rules, as well as what customs forms are required, size restrictions, and labeling requirements. You can check their list at http://pe.usps.com/text/imm/ab_toc.htm. There are two main customs forms: PS Form 2976 and PS Form 2976A. The former is generally used for mail that is valued under $400 and the latter is for mail valued over $400. For more information on which forms to use and how to fill them out, consult www.usps.com/send/customs-forms.htm.

INSURANCE: TO BUY OR NOT TO BUY?

Unless your baked goods are gilded with gold or encrusted with diamonds, it's not worth insuring your packages. With the money spent insuring the box and the time it would take to file an insurance claim if something happened to it, you could probably easily whip up a replacement batch of cookies and brownies.

A FEW MORE POINTS ABOUT SHIPPING . . .

- Consider shipping by air instead of ground for quicker arrivals and a smoother ride.

- Winter and summer are dicier times to send food because of the possibility of extreme weather conditions. If anything needs to be under temperature control, use a Styrofoam shipping container with freezer packs (if appropriate) and ship as quickly as you can.

- Let your loved one know to expect something in the mail. Even if it spoils the surprise a little, it's more important to let recipients know that there's something on the way. And if they'll be away, they can make arrangements for someone to pick it up.

- Don't forget to verify addresses, as errors can create delays in delivery.

- College mailrooms may take an extra day to process packages for students. Keep this in mind when selecting treats to include in packages.

- Many summer camps have strict policies regarding care packages, so be sure to double-check their rules on food items. Some camps restrict sweets and other treats because they may attract insects; others prohibit food altogether because of food allergies.

- Dry ice is considered a hazardous material and must be declared when shipping. None of the recipes in this book require dry ice, but for the adventurous among you who ship highly perishable foods, just be aware that carriers need to know.

SENDING TO A SOLDIER

According to the U.S. government, there were more than 1.4 million personnel on active duty in the Armed Forces in 2011. This counts those in the Army, Air Force, Navy, Coast Guard, and Marine Corps. For these troops, especially those stationed far away, nothing can be more comforting than receiving a taste of home. Sending a package to someone in the Armed Forces requires a bit more effort, but it's not difficult once you know what and how to ship, and what restrictions each country may have (remember that packages going through military mail are still subject to mail restrictions just like nonmilitary packages).

Addressing Mili-Mail

Years ago, the DOD and the USPS partnered in developing Overseas Military Mail to facilitate the delivery of mail to military personnel overseas. In doing so, they developed a scheme for addressing mail that is slightly modified from how we address civilian mail in the United States. This helps the USPS's machines properly sort and then transfer the mail to the correct processing facility, where it then gets further sorted and distributed before arriving at its correct destination.

For the military, the scheme looks like this (note that there are city and state equivalents that must be used):

> Name
> Postal Service Center + Identifier
> APO/FPO/DPO + AA/AE/AP + ZIP

The three City equivalents are:

> APO: Army Post Office
> FPO: Fleet Post Office
> DPO: Diplomatic Post Office

The three State equivalents are:

> AA: Armed Forces Americas (includes Central and South America and the Caribbean)
>
> AE: Armed Forces Europe (includes Canada, Africa, and the Middle East)
>
> AP: Armed Forces Pacific (includes Asia and the Pacific region)

Once your loved one receives his or her military address, record it someplace where it won't get lost. Although there are ways of locating people on active duty, it may be an arduous process, so save yourself the time and effort.

Mailing Through the USPS

Because of the mail agreement between the USPS and DOD, the USPS provides postal service to all personnel and families of the Armed Forces worldwide. Their policy is to provide the same level of service to the military as if they were living in the United States. Therefore, the price of mailing Military Mail is the same as for domestic postage, regardless of where the personnel are stationed. Mail with APO/FPO/DPO addresses is not considered international mail, but the transit times will reflect international mail depending on the distance they are traveling. The Military Mail section of the USPS website has a handy chart that estimates the number of days it takes for mail to be delivered. This is an important consideration when selecting perishables for shipping to military personnel. Neither FedEx nor UPS can ship directly to APO/FPO/DPO addresses.

However, note that packages going through military and diplomatic mail are still subject to mail restrictions that may go beyond country-specific ones. The USPS has an extensive list based on APO/FPO/DPO ZIP codes that can be checked here: http://about.usps.com/postal-bulletin/2012/pb22338/html/apo.htm.

To help with mailing, the USPS offers free "Mili-Kits" that you can request via phone (1-800-610-8734); you cannot order the kits online. When you reach an agent, request "CAREKIT04" or tell them you would like the military kit. It can take 7 to 10 days for the kit to get delivered. The kit has supplies that military families frequently request and includes Priority Mail boxes and labels, and customs forms and envelopes.

Preparing Your Military Care Package

Creating a care package for someone in the Armed Forces is similar to creating a package for someone in the United States. However, because the conditions abroad may be a little different, here are some helpful tips to consider when sending a package to a soldier.

- Pack treats in zipper-top plastic bags to protect them from the elements, such as sand and rain.

- Avoid using Styrofoam packing peanuts. Because of the heat, the static cling that's created with the peanuts may make cleanup particularly difficult.

- Use strong, reinforced materials to package treats, as they must travel far and endure a lot of handling.

- Some ingredients may not hold up to extreme temperatures or desert heat:

  — Butter, margarine, peanut butter, and nuts may be more susceptible to spoilage or rancidity. Butter-flavored vegetable shortening is a good alternative to butter and margarine in such cases.

  — Brown sugar, corn syrup, or molasses may cause baked goods to get moldy because of their water content. White granulated sugar may be a better option.

  — Chocolate may melt if it's used as a topping or coating. Baking chocolate into a treat can help avoid this potential problem.

Other Tips and Considerations

Ship care packages by Priority Mail, as it travels by air rather than by water. Even so, depending on where a soldier is stationed, it can take 7 to 14 days for a package to get delivered through Priority Mail.

- Mail tracking service is available if an extra service such as registered mail, delivery confirmation, or insurance is purchased for the package. However, sending a package registered or insured may be a hassle for some soldiers because they must go to base camp to pick it up. If the package isn't valuable, it might not be worth the bother.

- List the mailing address on both the outside and the inside of the box. Use the soldier's full name (do not put rank), unit, and APO/FPO/DPO address. Do not forget to include a return address.

- Do not put the country or base camp city on the package. If you do, it may end up going through that country's mail system rather than the military.

- Mail must be addressed to specific soldiers. In the past, people could address mail to "Any Soldier" or "Any Service Member," but due to security concerns, this is no longer allowed.

- Don't forget to fill out customs forms!

SO WHAT'S NEXT?

Now that we've covered the history of care packages, discussed what baked goods are suitable for shipping, and gone over the ins and outs of packing and shipping, it's time to get your mixing bowls and measuring cups and spoons ready! The following chapters include some of my favorite goodies that I send to friends and family. Whether you bake a traditional brownie or whip up a savory snack, your loved ones will surely be impressed when any of these tasty treats arrive on their doorsteps.

high-flying BROWNIES and BARS

Whether you are shipping to a nearby city or locales around the world, brownies and bars are lusty treats that can stand up to bumpy roads and rough conditions. Sturdy and dense, these goodies practically beg to be held for long periods and often taste better over time. Wrap the bars individually with plastic wrap, cellophane, parchment paper, or waxed paper, and then seal with tape or a sticker. Pack the wrapped treats in a zipper-top plastic bag or, for a more festive look, neatly arrange them in a decorative tin—this also allows your recipient to share the treats more easily. Alternatively, you may layer unwrapped bars in an airtight container with the layers separated by waxed or parchment paper.

Rocky Road Brownies *with a* Twist

The "twist" in this rich and chewy treat are the pretzel twists that are scattered on top. The pretzels add a few more "bumps in the road" as well as a salty element to help balance out the sweet marshmallows and chocolate chips. Individually wrap each brownie to prevent the marshmallows from sticking. These brownies are a good choice for care packages that need to travel for up to 7 days. **MAKES 16 BROWNIES**

- 8 tablespoons (1 stick) unsalted butter
- 4 ounces unsweetened chocolate
- 1¼ cups sugar
- ¼ teaspoon salt
- 1 teaspoon pure vanilla extract
- 2 large eggs, at room temperature
- 1 cup all-purpose flour
- 2 tablespoons natural unsweetened cocoa powder
- ⅓ cup toasted chopped walnuts (see page 95)
- 1 cup mini pretzel twists (about 20 pretzels)
- 1 cup miniature marshmallows
- ¼ cup semisweet chocolate chips

1. Preheat the oven to 350°F. Grease and flour an 8-inch square pan or line with parchment paper; set aside.

2. Put the butter and chocolate in a medium-size heatproof bowl. Set the bowl over a pot of simmering water and stir until the butter and chocolate are melted and blended. Remove the bowl from the heat and stir in the sugar, salt, and vanilla. Set aside to begin cooling.

3. While the mixture is still slightly warm, add the eggs. Stir until well blended. Mix in the flour and cocoa, and then stir in the walnuts. Transfer the mixture to the prepared pan and then top with the pretzel twists. Bake for 25 minutes.

4. Remove the brownies from the oven, top with the marshmallows and chocolate chips, and return the pan to the oven for another 5 minutes, or until a toothpick inserted into the brownies comes out with just a few crumbs clinging to it.

5. Let the brownies cool completely in the pan on a rack. Using a serrated knife, slice into 16 squares. Wrap the brownies individually with waxed or parchment paper or plastic wrap, seal with tape, and pack in a zipper-top plastic bag or other container. Alternatively, layer unwrapped bars in an airtight container, separating the layers with waxed or parchment paper.

Pecan Sandy Bars

A variation on the classic cookie, these bars are rich, buttery, and nutty—perfect for those who crave a mellower sweet treat. Because these bars are dry, they can be packed loosely in food-safe tins without going stale—great for long-distance friends and family. I once packed them up for a journey across the country and they kept for more than 2 weeks. **MAKES 16 BARS**

1. Line an 8-inch square pan with parchment paper, leaving extra for over-hang; set aside. Combine the flour and salt in a medium-size bowl.

2. In the bowl of an electric mixer, beat the butter and sugar on medium speed until light and fluffy, scraping the sides of the bowl occasionally. Add the vanilla and mix until combined. Mix in the dry ingredients and then fold in the chopped pecans. Transfer the mixture to the prepared pan and press firmly into the bottom of the pan. Chill for at least 30 minutes in the refrigerator.

3. Meanwhile, preheat the oven to 300°F. Remove the pan from the refrigerator and lightly score the surface of the dough to create sixteen 2-inch squares. Bake until the bars are golden brown on the edges, 45 minutes to 1 hour.

4. Let cool in the pan on a rack. While the bars are still a bit warm, grasp the edges of the parchment paper and lift the bars out of the pan. Using a sharp knife, cut along the scored lines. Transfer the squares to the rack to cool completely. Wrap the bars individually with waxed or parchment paper or plastic wrap, seal with tape, and pack in a zipper-top plastic bag or other container. Alternatively, layer unwrapped bars in an airtight container, separating the layers with waxed or parchment paper.

2 cups all-purpose flour

1 teaspoon kosher salt

1 cup (2 sticks) unsalted butter, at room temperature

¾ cup confectioners' sugar

½ teaspoon pure vanilla extract

1 cup toasted chopped pecans (see page 95)

Dream Bars

I use chocolate cookie crumbs instead of the traditional graham crackers in these dream bars because I love the rich, dark, and slightly bitter flavor of the chocolate. For the crumbs, I scrape the creme filling off chocolate sandwich cookies (you could also use chocolate wafer cookies) and then place them in a zipper-top plastic bag. I then crush them with a rolling pin. These decadent (and dreamy!) treats are best individually wrapped and then placed in a sturdy container before packing. They hold up well during shipping and will keep for more than 1 week. **MAKES 16 BARS**

1 cup chocolate cookie crumbs (from sandwich cookies or chocolate wafer cookies)

4 tablespoons (½ stick) salted butter, melted

½ cup semisweet chocolate chips or chunks

¼ cup peanut butter chips

¼ cup white chocolate chips

½ cup toasted chopped pecans or almonds (see page 95)

1 cup unsweetened shredded coconut

¾ cup sweetened condensed milk

1. Preheat the oven to 350°F. Line an 8-inch square pan with parchment paper or foil, leaving some extra for overhang; set aside.

2. In a medium-size bowl, combine the cookie crumbs with the melted butter. Using a spatula, mix thoroughly, making sure that all the crumbs get coated with butter. Transfer the crumbs to the prepared pan and, using the bottom of a measuring cup, press the crumbs into the bottom of the pan. Bake for 10 minutes. Transfer the pan to a rack to cool for 20 minutes.

3. Meanwhile, in a medium-size bowl, combine the semisweet chocolate chips, peanut butter chips, white chocolate chips, nuts, and coconut. Stir to combine. Evenly distribute the mixture over the cooled crust and then drizzle the condensed milk on top. Return the pan to the oven and bake until the top is golden brown, 20 to 25 minutes.

4. Let cool in the pan on a rack. Remove the bars from the pan by grasping the edges of the parchment paper, and cut into 16 squares. Wrap the bars individually with waxed or parchment paper or plastic wrap, seal with tape, and pack in a zipper-top plastic bag or other container. Alternatively, layer unwrapped bars in an airtight container, separating the layers with waxed or parchment paper.

Butterscotch Blondies

The old-timey flavor of butterscotch brings me back to my childhood, when I used to find the flavored pudding in my packed lunches or serve myself dollops of it from salad bars. These days, I occasionally treat myself to butterscotch in the form of this goodie. Send this packable sweet to people from your youth, such as an old friend or even a teacher who made a difference in your life. These blondies will stand up to the rigors of transit and keep for at least a week. **MAKES 24 BLONDIES**

12 tablespoons (1½ sticks) unsalted butter

1½ cups packed light brown sugar

1½ cups all-purpose flour

2 teaspoons baking powder

½ teaspoon salt

3 large eggs, at room temperature

2 teaspoons pure vanilla extract

⅔ cup butterscotch chips

⅓ cup white chocolate chips

1. Preheat the oven to 350°F. Grease and flour a 9 x 13-inch pan or line with parchment paper; set aside.

2. In a medium-size saucepan over medium-low heat, combine the butter and brown sugar. Stir until the butter is melted and the sugar is dissolved. Remove from the heat and set aside to begin cooling.

3. In a medium-size bowl, combine the flour, baking powder, and salt.

4. While the butter and sugar mixture is still warm to the touch, add the eggs and vanilla. Stir until combined. Add the dry ingredients and mix until blended. Fold in half of the butterscotch chips and half of the white chocolate chips. Pour the batter into the prepared pan. Scatter the remaining chips on top. Bake until a toothpick inserted into the center of the blondies comes out clean, 22 to 27 minutes.

5. Let cool in the pan on a rack before cutting into 24 bars. Wrap the bars individually with waxed or parchment paper or plastic wrap, seal with tape, and pack in a zipper-top plastic bag or other container. Alternatively, layer unwrapped bars in an airtight container, separating the layers with waxed or parchment paper.

Size Matters

Cookies and bars will ship better if you keep them on the smaller side and make them at least ¼ inch thick. With a small, sturdy size, there will be less opportunity for breakage.

Chocolate-Cherry Brownies

I love the flavors of chocolate and cherries, so I put them together in this rich and decadent brownie, which holds up very well for long and bumpy trips and will keep for up to 2 weeks. The cherries lend moisture, a slightly tart flavor, and a chewy texture to keep the treats from tasting stale. After about a week, the brownies will develop a crunchy exterior yet still have a moist and fudgy interior. **MAKES 16 BROWNIES**

1. Preheat the oven to 350°F. Line an 8-inch square pan with parchment paper, leaving extra for overhang; set aside.

2. In a medium-size saucepan over low heat, combine the butter, sugar, cocoa, and salt. Whisk together until melted and combined; remove from the heat and set aside to begin cooling.

3. While the butter mixture is still a bit warm, add the eggs and vanilla. Stir together until the batter becomes thick and glossy. Mix in the flour and stir until combined. Fold in the cherries.

4. Spread the mixture in the prepared pan. Bake until a toothpick inserted in the center comes out with small crumbs clinging to it, 33 to 35 minutes.

5. Let cool in the pan on a rack. Remove the brownies from the pan by grasping the edges of the parchment paper, and cut into 16 squares. Wrap the bars individually with waxed or parchment paper or plastic wrap, seal with tape, and pack in a zipper-top plastic bag or other container. Alternatively, layer unwrapped bars in an airtight container, separating the layers with waxed or parchment paper.

10 tablespoons (1¼ sticks) unsalted butter

1¼ cups sugar

¾ cup Dutch-processed cocoa powder

¼ teaspoon kosher salt

2 large eggs, at room temperature

½ teaspoon pure vanilla extract

½ cup all-purpose flour

¾ cup dried tart cherries

Chewy Hermit Bars

Perfect for holiday care packages, these bars will endure a long journey well because of the molasses and dried fruit, which help keep the bars moist and chewy. Best of all, though, they even improve in flavor over time. Pack them as directed below and they'll keep for 2 weeks. MAKES 32 BARS

2 cups all-purpose flour

½ teaspoon baking powder

½ teaspoon baking soda

½ teaspoon salt

½ teaspoon ground cinnamon

¼ teaspoon ground nutmeg

¼ teaspoon ground allspice

8 tablespoons (1 stick) unsalted butter, at room temperature

½ cup sugar

2 large eggs, at room temperature

½ cup molasses

1 cup dried mixed fruit, such as cranberries, raisins, and/or chopped apricots

¼ cup crystallized ginger (optional)

½ cup chopped toasted hazelnuts or almonds (see page 95)

Sparkling sugar (optional)

1. Preheat the oven to 350°F. Line a large rimmed baking sheet with parchment paper or a silicone baking liner; set aside.

2. In a medium-size bowl, combine the flour, baking powder, baking soda, salt, cinnamon, nutmeg, and allspice.

3. In the bowl of an electric mixer, beat the butter and sugar on medium speed until light and fluffy. Add the eggs and molasses; mix until combined. Gradually add the flour mixture to the molasses mixture and mix for a minute or two. Fold in the dried fruit, crystallized ginger (if using), and the nuts.

4. Transfer the dough to the prepared baking sheet. Spread into a 9 x 12-inch rectangle about ½ inch thick. Sprinkle with sparkling sugar, if desired. Bake until the edges begin to brown, about 15 minutes.

5. Let cool in the pan on a rack before slicing into 32 bars. Wrap the bars individually with waxed or parchment paper or plastic wrap, seal with tape, and pack in a zipper-top plastic bag or other container. Alternatively, layer unwrapped bars in an airtight container, separating the layers with waxed or parchment paper.

Peanut Butter Crunch Brownies

I don't know whose idea it was to put chocolate and peanut butter together, but I'm glad someone thought of it! I like to cut these nutty brownies into squares or use cookie cutters to make interesting or more individualized shapes. I pack them in tins or stack them in cellophane bags secured with raffia or ribbon before shipping. They are a good choice for short, quick shipping, as they keep for up to 5 days. **MAKES 16 BROWNIES**

1. Preheat the oven to 350°F. Grease and flour an 8-inch square pan or line with parchment paper; set aside.

2. Put the butter and chocolate in a medium-size heatproof bowl. Set the bowl over a pot of simmering water and stir until the butter and chocolate are melted and blended. Remove the bowl from the heat and stir in the sugar and salt; mix to combine. Set aside to begin cooling.

3. While the mixture is still slightly warm, add the eggs one at a time, stirring after each one to incorporate fully, and then add the vanilla. Fold in the flour and cocoa, and mix until there are no streaks.

4. Put the peanut butter in a small bowl. Microwave on high power for 10 to 15 seconds or until the peanut butter is loose and runny. Fold the peanut butter into the brownie batter, leaving some streaks. Pour the batter into the prepared pan and then scatter the peanuts on top. Bake until a toothpick inserted into the center of the pan comes out mostly clean (some crumbs are okay), about 30 minutes.

5. Allow the brownies to cool in the pan on a rack before slicing into 16 squares. Wrap the brownies individually with waxed or parchment paper or plastic wrap, seal with tape, and pack in a zipper-top plastic bag or other container. Alternatively, layer unwrapped bars in an airtight container, separating the layers with waxed or parchment paper. These brownies also ship well stacked in cellophane bags, which you can tie closed with string or ribbon.

8 tablespoons (1 stick) unsalted butter

4 ounces unsweetened chocolate

1¼ cups sugar

¼ teaspoon salt

2 large eggs, at room temperature

1 teaspoon pure vanilla extract

1 cup all-purpose flour

2 tablespoons natural unsweetened cocoa powder

½ cup creamy or crunchy peanut butter

½ cup crushed lightly salted peanuts

Almond, Fig, *and* Apricot Squares

Packaged in cans or tubes, almond paste is made primarily from ground almonds and sugar, and it is typically used in dessert fillings. I love it in this recipe because it keeps the squares nice and moist and imparts a delicate almond flavor. Almond paste can be found in most supermarkets in the baking aisle. It should not be confused with marzipan, which is an almond-based candy dough that contains a higher amount of sugar. These squares will keep for up to 2 weeks. **MAKES 16 SQUARES**

1. Preheat the oven to 350°F. Grease and flour an 8-inch square pan or line with parchment paper; set aside.

2. In a small saucepan over medium heat, melt the butter. When brown specks begin to form on the bottom of the pan and the butter releases a nutty aroma, immediately remove the pan from the heat. Stir in the brown sugar and both extracts, and set aside to begin cooling.

3. In a medium-size bowl, combine the flour, baking powder, and salt. While the butter mixture is still slightly warm, add the egg and stir to incorporate. Add the flour mixture and stir again. Fold in the figs, apricots, and almond paste. Pour the batter into the prepared pan and bake until a toothpick inserted into the center of the squares comes out clean, about 25 minutes.

4. Let cool in the pan before slicing into 16 squares. Wrap the bars individually with waxed or parchment paper or plastic wrap, seal with tape, and pack in a zipper-top plastic bag or other container. Alternatively, layer unwrapped bars in an airtight container, separating the layers with waxed or parchment paper.

8 tablespoons (1 stick) unsalted butter

¾ cup packed light brown sugar

1 teaspoon pure almond extract

¼ teaspoon pure vanilla extract

1 cup all-purpose flour

1 teaspoon baking powder

¼ teaspoon salt

1 large egg, at room temperature

½ cup chopped dried figs

¼ cup chopped dried apricots

½ cup almond paste (not marzipan), broken into bite-size chunks

Walnut-Maple Blondies

When I was growing up in New England, there was no shortage of maple syrup to go around. In supermarkets and gift shops, you could find maple leaf–shaped bottles filled with the amber liquid, as well as maple-flavored fudge, lollipops, and sugar. There are two major grades of maple syrup in the United States: Grade A and Grade B. Grade A is considered superior to B, but the latter, which is thicker and darker, is preferable in this recipe because it has a richer maple flavor. These treats make for a great gift during the fall season to friends and family on both coasts—ship them as soon as they are baked and cooled, since they keep for only 5 days. **MAKES 16 BLONDIES**

½ cup walnut halves

½ cup plus 1 tablespoon pure maple syrup

Pinch of kosher salt

1 cup all-purpose flour

½ teaspoon baking powder

¼ teaspoon salt

8 tablespoons (1 stick) unsalted butter

½ cup packed light brown sugar

1 large egg, at room temperature

1. Combine the walnuts, 1 tablespoon of the maple syrup, and the kosher salt in a small skillet over medium-high heat. Stir the mixture until the maple syrup begins to crystallize. Remove from the heat and pour the nuts onto a baking sheet to cool.

2. Preheat the oven to 350°F. Grease and flour an 8-inch square pan or line with parchment paper; set aside.

3. In a medium-size bowl, combine the flour, baking powder, and salt.

4. In the bowl of an electric mixer, beat the butter and brown sugar on medium speed until light and fluffy. Add the remaining ½ cup maple syrup and the egg. Mix for another minute or until combined. Add the flour mixture and mix on low speed until blended.

5. Coarsely chop the walnuts into small pieces and fold half of the nuts into the batter. Pour the batter into the prepared pan and scatter the remaining walnuts on top. Bake until a toothpick inserted into the center of the blondies comes out clean, about 30 minutes.

6. Let cool in the pan on a rack before cutting into 16 squares. Wrap the bars individually with waxed or parchment paper or plastic wrap, seal with tape, and pack in a zipper-top plastic bag or other container. Alternatively, layer unwrapped bars in an airtight container, separating the layers with waxed or parchment paper.

Chewy Gooey Blondies

A cousin to the traditional chocolate brownie, the blondie is a rich bar cookie based on the flavor of brown sugar and butter. In this recipe, I've intensified the flavor by browning the butter, a simple process that yields a nutty flavor and aroma. Ship 'em to your kids at school—preferably overnight, as they keep for 5 days—and they'll probably call you asking for more. **MAKES 16 BLONDIES**

1. Preheat the oven to 350°F. Grease and flour an 8-inch square pan or line with parchment paper; set aside.

2. In a small saucepan over medium heat, melt the butter. When brown specks begin to form on the bottom of the pan and the butter releases a nutty aroma, immediately remove the pan from the heat. Stir in the brown sugar and vanilla; set aside to begin cooling.

3. In a medium-size bowl, combine the flour, baking powder, baking soda, and salt. While the butter mixture is still slightly warm, add the egg and stir to incorporate. Add the flour mixture and stir again. Fold in the chocolate chips. Pour the batter into the prepared pan and bake until a toothpick inserted into the center of the squares comes out nearly clean, 20 to 25 minutes.

4. Let cool in the pan before slicing into 16 squares. Wrap the bars individually with waxed or parchment paper or plastic wrap, seal with tape, and pack in a zipper-top plastic bag or other container. Alternatively, layer unwrapped bars in an airtight container, separating the layers with waxed or parchment paper.

8 tablespoons (1 stick) unsalted butter

1 cup packed light brown sugar

1½ teaspoon pure vanilla extract

1 cup all-purpose flour

½ teaspoon baking powder

⅛ teaspoon baking soda

¼ teaspoon salt

1 large egg, at room temperature

½ cup semisweet chocolate chips

Cherry Crumble Bars

These rich, buttery bars are the perfect combination of sweet, tart, and salty. Instead of using a shortbread base, I use oats to give the bars some extra texture, heft, and flavor. Individually wrapped or packed in a tin, these bars are a good choice for short transit times; they will stay fresh for 7 days. **MAKES 16 BARS**

- 8 tablespoons (1 stick) unsalted butter, at room temperature
- ½ cup granulated sugar
- ½ cup packed light brown sugar
- 1 teaspoon pure almond extract
- ¼ teaspoon pure vanilla extract
- 1 cup all-purpose flour
- 1 cup old-fashioned rolled oats
- ½ teaspoon salt
- ½ teaspoon ground cinnamon
- 1 cup good-quality red cherry preserves, such as Hero brand

1. Preheat the oven to 350°F. Line an 8-inch square pan with parchment paper, leaving extra for overhang; set aside.

2. In the bowl of an electric mixer, beat the butter and sugars on medium speed until light and fluffy. Add both extracts and mix again until combined. Add the flour, oats, salt, and cinnamon; mix on low speed until combined. The mixture should be loose and somewhat crumbly.

3. Press two-thirds of the mixture firmly into the bottom of the prepared pan. With a knife or offset spatula, spread the preserves on top. Scatter the remaining crumb mixture over the top. Bake until the preserves are bubbly and the crust is golden brown, 30 to 35 minutes.

4. Let cool in the pan. Remove the bars from the pan by grasping the edges of the parchment paper, and cut into 16 squares. Wrap the bars individually with waxed or parchment paper or plastic wrap, seal with tape, and pack in a zipper-top plastic bag or other container. Alternatively, layer unwrapped bars in an airtight container, separating the layers with waxed or parchment paper. These bars also do well stacked in cellophane bags tied closed with a ribbon.

Making Crusts

Measuring cups come in handy when you have to press a loose crumb mixture such as shortbread into a pan. Use a measuring cup to evenly distribute the crumbs in the bottom of the pan and then use the bottom of the cup to press the crumbs into a solid layer.

Cranberry-Pumpkin Seed Bars

This whole-grain snack takes advantage of the flavors of fall with the combination of cranberries and pumpkin seeds. They stay moist and chewy for about 10 days and travel extremely well, tolerating both extreme heat and cold. MAKES 12 BARS

2 cups old-fashioned rolled oats

1 cup hulled raw pumpkin seeds

1 cup dried cranberries

Pinch of salt

6 tablespoons vegetable or canola oil

¼ cup honey

¼ cup light corn syrup

¼ cup pure maple syrup

½ teaspoon pure vanilla extract

1. Preheat the oven to 350°F. Line two 5 x 9-inch loaf pans with parchment paper, leaving extra for overhang; set aside.

2. In a medium-size bowl, combine the oats, pumpkin seeds, cranberries, and salt.

3. In a heavy-bottomed medium-size saucepan over medium heat, heat the oil, honey, corn syrup, and maple syrup. When the mixture comes to a simmer, remove the pan from the heat and stir in the vanilla. Pour the mixture over the oat mixture. Using a heatproof spatula, stir until the oats are completely coated. Pour the oat mixture into the prepared pans and firmly press into the bottom of the pans. Bake until the edges begin to brown, 20 to 25 minutes.

4. Let cool in the pans on a rack. While the bars are still slightly warm, remove from the pans by lifting the edges of the parchment paper. Cut each loaf crosswise into 6 bars, for a total of 12 bars, and transfer to the rack to cool completely. Wrap the bars individually with waxed or parchment paper or plastic wrap, seal with tape, and pack in a zipper-top plastic bag or other container. Alternatively, layer unwrapped bars in an airtight container, separating the layers with waxed or parchment paper.

Apricot-Pecan Bars

The chewy apricots, honey, and jam keep this treat moist for up to 10 days. Package the bars stacked in cellophane bags tied with a ribbon if you are shipping them shorter distances, or layer them in cookie tins for longer distances. **MAKES 16 BARS**

1. Preheat the oven to 350°F. Line an 8-inch square pan with parchment paper, leaving extra for overhang; set aside.

2. In the bowl of a food processor, combine the pecans and flour. Process until the pecans are ground up finely into the flour. Add the sugar and salt, and pulse a few times. Add the butter and process until the mixture becomes crumbly. Transfer three-quarters of the crumb mixture to the prepared pan and firmly press into the bottom of the pan. Refrigerate the remaining crumb mixture. Prick the crust with a fork and bake in the oven until golden, about 25 minutes. Let cool on a rack for 10 to 15 minutes.

3. Meanwhile, place the dried apricots in a medium-size heatproof bowl and cover with boiling water. Allow the apricots to soak until they plump up, 20 to 25 minutes. Discard the water and transfer the apricots to the bowl of the food processor. Add ⅓ cup of the jam, the honey, and the vanilla. Process into a puree, adding more jam if necessary to create a smooth consistency.

4. Spread the apricot puree onto the cooled crust and sprinkle the reserved crumb mixture on top of the puree. Return the pan to the oven and bake until the crumb topping is light brown, about 20 minutes.

5. Let the bars cool for 10 minutes. Remove the bars from the pan by grasping the edges of the parchment paper. Cut into 16 squares and transfer to a rack to cool completely. Wrap the bars individually with waxed or parchment paper or plastic wrap, seal with tape, and pack in a zipper-top plastic bag or other container. Alternatively, layer unwrapped bars in an airtight container, separating the layers with waxed or parchment paper. You may also package these in cellophane bags tied closed with a ribbon.

¾ cup toasted pecans (see page 95)

1½ cups all-purpose flour

¾ cup sugar

½ teaspoon kosher salt

12 tablespoons (1½ sticks) unsalted butter, cut into small pieces

1½ cups dried apricots

⅓ to ½ cup apricot jam

1 tablespoon honey

½ teaspoon pure vanilla extract

Hunting and Gathering

Nothing is worse than getting halfway through a recipe and realizing that you're missing or don't have enough of something. It takes only a few minutes to read through a recipe completely and then gather all of your ingredients. Make sure to take a peek—and a sniff—inside each package to make sure you have enough and that it is still good.

Box Office Brownies

While these brownies don't include buttered popcorn, movie buffs and candy lovers will appreciate this treat that's made with the boxed candy found at movie theater concessions. Pack them up in a food-safe tin and send them with a pair of movie passes or some DVDs of past Oscar winners. They will keep for 5 days. **MAKES 16 BROWNIES**

1. Preheat the oven to 350°F. Grease and flour an 8-inch square pan or line with parchment paper; set aside.

2. Put the butter and chocolate in a medium-size heatproof bowl. Set the bowl over a pot of simmering water and melt the ingredients together, stirring occasionally. Remove the bowl from the heat. Add the sugar and salt and mix to combine; set aside to begin cooling. While the mixture is still slightly warm, add the eggs, one at a time, stirring after each one to incorporate fully, and then add the vanilla. Fold in the flour and cocoa, and mix until there are no streaks.

3. Fold half of the candy into the brownie batter. Pour the batter into the prepared pan and then scatter the remaining candy on top. Bake until a toothpick inserted into the center of the pan comes out mostly clean (some crumbs are okay), about 30 minutes.

4. Let the brownies cool in the pan before slicing into 16 squares. Wrap the bars individually with waxed or parchment paper or plastic wrap, seal with tape, and pack in a zipper-top plastic bag or other container. Alternatively, layer unwrapped bars in an airtight container, separating the layers with waxed or parchment paper.

8 tablespoons (1 stick) unsalted butter

4 ounces unsweetened chocolate

1¼ cups sugar

¼ teaspoon salt

2 large eggs, at room temperature

1 teaspoon pure vanilla extract

1 cup all-purpose flour

2 tablespoons natural unsweetened cocoa powder

¼ cup chocolate-covered raisins

¼ cup chocolate-covered peanuts

¼ cup nonpareil-coated chocolates

¼ cup candy-coated peanut butter candy pieces

Buzz! Buzz! Chocolate-Espresso Brownies

Help your favorite student perk up with this caffeinated treat that's flavored with espresso powder and chocolate-covered espresso beans. Choose beans that are covered with dark chocolate, as they have an intense coffee flavor and are not overly sweet. Pack up these treats during finals week to send to your beloved college student who may be pulling all-nighters. They will keep for 5 days—just long enough for a week of exams! **MAKES 16 BROWNIES**

8 tablespoons (1 stick) unsalted butter

4 ounces unsweetened chocolate

1 tablespoon instant espresso powder or instant coffee granules

1¼ cups sugar

¼ teaspoon salt

2 large eggs, at room temperature

1 cup all-purpose flour

1 cup chocolate-covered espresso or coffee beans

1. Preheat the oven to 350°F. Grease and flour an 8-inch square pan or line with parchment paper; set aside.

2. Put the butter, chocolate, and espresso powder in a medium-size heatproof bowl. Set the bowl over a pot of simmering water and melt the ingredients, stirring occasionally. Remove the bowl from the heat. Add the sugar and salt and mix to combine; set aside to begin cooling. While the mixture is still slightly warm, add the eggs one at a time, stirring after each one to incorporate fully. Fold in the flour and mix until there are no streaks.

3. Coarsely chop the espresso beans. Fold half of the beans into the brownie batter. Pour the batter into the prepared pan and top with the remaining espresso beans. Bake until a toothpick inserted into the center of the pan comes out mostly clean (some crumbs are okay), about 30 minutes.

4. Allow the brownies to cool in the pan before slicing into 16 squares. Wrap the bars individually with waxed or parchment paper or plastic wrap, seal with tape, and pack in a zipper-top plastic bag or other container. Alternatively, layer unwrapped bars in an airtight container, separating the layers with waxed or parchment paper.

High-Energy Peanut Bars

Perfect for late-afternoon energy lulls, these bars provide a combination of protein and carbohydrates that will satisfy someone on who's on the trail, in the car, or even in class. Using a mixture of shelf-stable ingredients, these bars absorb shocks well during shipping and keep for at least 1 week when packaged and stored properly. **MAKES 12 BARS**

1. Preheat the oven to 350°F. Line two 5 x 9-inch loaf pans with parchment paper, leaving extra for overhang; set aside.

2. In a medium-size bowl, combine the oats and peanuts.

3. In a small heavy-bottomed saucepan over medium heat, bring the corn syrup, honey, oil, and peanut butter to a simmer. Stir to ensure that the peanut butter is well incorporated. Remove from the heat and pour the mixture over the oats. Stir the oats until they are completely coated with the peanut butter mixture. Pour the mixture into the prepared pans and firmly press into the pans. Bake until the edges are golden brown, 20 to 25 minutes.

4. Allow the bars to cool in the pans. While they are still slightly warm, grasp the parchment paper and pull the bars out of the pans. Cut each loaf crosswise into 6 bars, for a total of 12 bars, and transfer to a rack to cool completely. Wrap the bars individually with waxed or parchment paper or plastic wrap, seal with tape, and pack in a zipper-top plastic bag or other container. Alternatively, layer unwrapped bars in an airtight container, separating the layers with waxed or parchment paper.

2 cups old-fashioned rolled oats

½ cup crushed lightly salted peanuts

6 tablespoons light corn syrup

6 tablespoons honey

¼ cup vegetable or canola oil

¼ cup creamy peanut butter

Blueberry-Flax Oat Bars

Inspired by one of my favorite cereals, these chewy granola bars include nuggets of dried blueberries and the nutty crunch of flax seeds. Flax seeds can be found in most larger supermarkets and in health food and specialty stores. They are a vegetarian source of omega-3 fatty acids, which have been found to be beneficial for the heart and brain. When stored properly, these bars will keep for 10 days. Ship them to health-conscious loved ones or to anyone who needs a healthy boost. **MAKES 12 BARS**

2 cups old-fashioned rolled oats

⅔ cup dried blueberries

2 tablespoons flax seeds

Pinch of salt

½ cup honey

6 tablespoons vegetable or canola oil

¼ cup pure maple syrup

½ teaspoon ground cinnamon

1. Preheat the oven to 350°F. Line two 5 x 9-inch loaf pans with parchment paper, leaving extra for overhang; set aside.

2. In a medium-size bowl, combine the oats, blueberries, flax seeds, and salt.

3. In a small, heavy-bottomed saucepan over medium heat, heat the honey, oil, and maple syrup. When the mixture comes to a simmer, remove the pan from the heat and stir in the cinnamon. Pour the mixture over the oat mixture. Using a heatproof spatula, stir until the oats are completely coated. Pour the mixture into the prepared pans and firmly press into the bottom of the pans. Bake until the edges begin to brown, 20 to 25 minutes.

4. Allow the bars to cool in the pans. While the bars are still slightly warm, grasp the parchment paper and lift the bars out of the pans. Cut each loaf crosswise into 6 bars, for a total of 12 bars, and transfer to a rack to cool completely. Wrap the bars individually with waxed or parchment paper or plastic wrap and seal with tape. Pack in a zipper-top plastic bag or container. Alternatively, layer unwrapped bars in an airtight container, separating the layers with waxed or parchment paper.

Banana-Cranberry Oat Bars

A cross between a granola bar and a cake, these treats are moist and chewy. Use any kind of dried fruit, such as raisins, blueberries, or cherries, if you don't have dried cranberries on hand, and ship them speedily, as they keep for only about 5 days. **MAKES 16 BARS**

1. Preheat the oven to 350°F. Grease and flour an 8-inch square pan or line with parchment paper; set aside.

2. In a medium-size bowl, combine the oats, flour, baking powder, and cinnamon.

3. In the bowl of an electric mixer, beat the butter and both sugars on medium speed until light and fluffy. Add the egg and vanilla, and mix again until blended. Add the oat mixture and mix on low speed until combined, scraping down the sides of the bowl if necessary. Fold in the banana and cranberries. Pour the batter into the prepared pan. Bake until a toothpick inserted into the center of the bars comes out clean, 25 to 28 minutes.

4. Let the bars cool in the pan for 10 minutes. Cut into 16 squares and transfer to a rack to cool completely. Wrap the bars individually with waxed or parchment paper or plastic wrap, seal with tape, and pack in a zipper-top plastic bag or other container. Alternatively, layer unwrapped bars in an airtight container, separating the layers with waxed or parchment paper.

½ cup old-fashioned rolled oats

⅓ cup all-purpose flour

1 teaspoon baking powder

½ teaspoon ground cinnamon

10 tablespoons (1¼ sticks) unsalted butter, at room temperature

¼ cup packed light brown sugar

¼ cup granulated sugar

1 large egg, at room temperature

1 teaspoon pure vanilla extract

¾ cup mashed ripe banana

½ cup dried cranberries

COOKIES *for the* ROAD

Cookies serve as the backbone of any care package. Not only do people love them, but their disk-like shape also makes them portable and the perfect handheld treat. This chapter includes traditional varieties, such as Chewy Oatmeal-Raisin Cookies and Classic Snickerdoodles, as well as some more unusual ones like ANZAC Biscuits and Herbes de Provence Cornmeal Cookies. To pack cookies, bundle them up in zipper-top plastic bags or airtight containers, packing any spaces with crumpled waxed paper to minimize shifting and potential breakage during transit. You may also assemble several cookies in a stack and enclose them in cellophane bags tied with ribbon for a more festive, professional touch.

Classic Snickerdoodles

In the sixth grade, one of my favorite classes was home economics, where I learned how to sew and bake. I loved the cooking portion so much that I still have the old mimeographed copies of the recipes that we made, including my very first cookie: the snickerdoodle. Pack these goodies in old cookie tins that you can purchase at antique stores to evoke a taste of nostalgia. They will keep for up to 1 week. **MAKES ABOUT 5 DOZEN COOKIES**

2¾ cups all-purpose flour

3 teaspoons baking powder

1 teaspoon ground cinnamon

Pinch of ground nutmeg

¼ teaspoon salt

1 cup (2 sticks) unsalted butter, at room temperature

2 cups sugar

2 large eggs, at room temperature

1 teaspoon pure vanilla extract

1. Preheat the oven to 350°F. Line two baking sheets with parchment paper or silicone baking liners; set aside.

2. In a medium-size bowl, combine the flour, baking powder, ½ teaspoon of the cinnamon, the nutmeg, and the salt.

3. In the bowl of an electric mixer, beat the butter and 1½ cups of the sugar on medium speed until light and fluffy. Add the eggs and vanilla to the butter mixture, and mix until blended. Add the flour mixture and mix on low speed until blended.

4. In a small bowl, combine the remaining ½ teaspoon cinnamon and ½ cup sugar. With your hands or a cookie dough scoop, form 1-inch balls with the dough. Roll the dough in the cinnamon sugar. Place the dough balls on the prepared baking sheets, about 2 inches apart. Bake until the edges begin to brown, 9 to 10 minutes.

5. Cool the cookies on the baking sheets for 5 minutes before transferring them to a rack to cool completely. Repeat with the remaining dough. Pack in zipper-top plastic bags, pressing out any air, or in airtight containers, separating the layers with waxed or parchment paper.

Malted Chocolate Chip Cookies

The secret to these cookies is the malt powder. Made from barley, wheat, and milk, this sweetener gives the cookies a somewhat nutty, *what-is-that?* flavor. Malt powder is different from malt drink mixes such as Horlicks and Ovaltine, which contain extra flavorings. You can find malted milk powder in the coffee and tea aisle in most supermarkets. I like to package these up in stacks of 5 in cellophane bags. I either use twist ties or ribbons to secure the bags before putting them in care packages for quick shipping (they keep for 5 days). **MAKES ABOUT 4 DOZEN COOKIES**

1. Preheat the oven to 350°F. Line two baking sheets with parchment paper or silicone baking liners; set aside.

2. In a medium-size bowl, combine the flour, malt powder, baking soda, and salt.

3. In the bowl of an electric mixer, beat the butter and both sugars on medium speed until light and fluffy. Add the egg, egg yolk, and vanilla, and mix until blended, scraping down the sides of the bowl if necessary. Add the flour mixture and mix on low speed until combined. Fold in the chocolate chips.

4. Using your hands or a cookie dough scoop, form 1-inch balls with the dough. Place the dough balls on the prepared baking sheets, about 2 inches apart. Bake until the edges of the cookies are lightly browned, 9 to 10 minutes. They will look slightly underdone in the centers.

5. Cool the cookies on the pans for 5 minutes before transferring them to a rack to cool completely. Repeat with the remaining dough. Pack in zipper-top plastic bags, pressing out any air, or in airtight containers, separating the layers with waxed or parchment paper. Alternatively, stack in cellophane bags tied with twist ties or ribbons.

2 cups all-purpose flour

⅓ cup malted milk powder (not malt drink mix)

½ teaspoon baking soda

½ teaspoon salt

12 tablespoons (1½ sticks) unsalted butter, melted

1 cup packed light brown sugar

¼ cup granulated sugar

1 large egg, at room temperature

1 large egg yolk, at room temperature

1 teaspoon pure vanilla extract

1 cup semisweet chocolate chips

Let It Rest

If possible, refrigerate the dough for at least 12 hours before baking; this will deepen the flavor.

Double-Ginger Molasses Cookies

Moist and chewy, these cookies get their intense flavor from a double dose of ginger—ground and crystallized. They are perfect as holiday gifts for friends and family, so look for seasonal-themed tins, wrapping, and containers for packaging these cookies. They'll keep for up to 1 week and even improve in flavor. **MAKES ABOUT 3 DOZEN COOKIES**

2¼ cups all-purpose flour

1 teaspoon baking soda

2 teaspoons ground ginger

½ teaspoon ground cinnamon

¼ teaspoon salt

12 tablespoons (1½ sticks) unsalted butter, at room temperature

1 cup sugar

1 large egg, at room temperature

¼ cup molasses

¼ cup chopped crystallized ginger

1. Preheat the oven to 350°F. Line two baking sheets with parchment paper or silicone baking liners; set aside.

2. In a medium-size bowl, combine the flour, baking soda, ground ginger, cinnamon, and salt.

3. In the bowl of an electric mixer, beat the butter and ¾ cup of the sugar on medium speed until light and fluffy. Add the egg and molasses; mix until blended, scraping down the sides of the bowl if necessary. Add the flour mixture and mix on low speed until just combined. Fold in the crystallized ginger.

4. Put the remaining ¼ cup sugar in a small bowl. With your hands or a cookie dough scoop, form the dough into 1-inch balls. Drop the balls into the sugar and roll to coat. Place the dough balls on the prepared baking sheets, about 2 inches apart. Bake until the edges are firm and the tops look crackly, 10 to 12 minutes.

5. Cool the cookies on the pans for 5 minutes before transferring them to a rack to cool completely. Repeat with the remaining dough. Pack in zipper-top plastic bags, pressing out any air, or in airtight containers, separating the layers with waxed or parchment paper.

Grasshopper Sandwich Cookies

This treat is reminiscent of a cookie that was one of my favorites when I was younger. The cookies will be crisp when you first make them but will soften the longer they sit, transforming into an irresistibly dense, cakey, soft cookie. They keep for 2 weeks, so they're perfect candidates for shipping. **MAKES ABOUT 2 DOZEN COOKIES**

COOKIES

- ¾ cup all-purpose flour, plus more for rolling
- ⅓ cup Dutch-processed cocoa powder, sifted
- ¼ teaspoon salt
- 6 tablespoons (¾ stick) unsalted butter, at room temperature
- ⅔ cup confectioners' sugar, sifted
- ¼ teaspoon instant espresso powder or coffee granules
- 1 large egg, at room temperature
- ½ teaspoon pure vanilla extract

PEPPERMINT FILLING

- 2 tablespoons vegetable shortening
- 2 tablespoons unsalted butter, at room temperature
- ¾ cup confectioners' sugar, sifted
- ¼ teaspoon peppermint extract
- 2 to 3 drops of green food coloring (optional)

1. Make the cookies: In a medium-size bowl, combine the flour, cocoa, and salt.

2. In the bowl of an electric mixer, beat the butter, sugar, and espresso powder on medium speed until light and fluffy. Add the egg and vanilla, and mix until combined. Add the flour mixture and mix on low speed until combined. Divide the dough in half and form into 2 disks. Wrap each in plastic wrap and refrigerate for at least 1 hour.

3. Meanwhile, make the filling: Put the shortening and butter in a medium-size bowl. Using a handheld mixer, blend them together. Add the sugar, extract, and food coloring (if using), and mix on low speed until combined; set aside.

4. Preheat the oven to 325°F. Line two baking sheets with parchment paper or silicone baking liners; set aside.

5. Using a rolling pin, roll out the dough to a ⅛-inch thickness, using extra flour if necessary to prevent the dough from sticking. Use 1½-inch round cutters to cut cookies out of the dough. Place the cookies on the prepared baking sheets, about 1 inch apart. Reroll the dough scraps and cut out more cookies. Bake until the edges of the cookies feel dry and firm, 10 to 12 minutes.

6. Cool the cookies for 5 minutes before transferring to a rack to cool completely. Repeat with the remaining dough. Spread a thin layer of filling on the underside of half of the cookies and top with another cookie to form a sandwich. Pack in zipper-top plastic bags, pressing out any air, or in airtight containers, separating the layers with waxed or parchment paper.

Crunchy PB & J Cookies

These lunch box–inspired cookies are crisp and slightly chewy when they first come out of the oven, but they will soften after a day or two. I like to pack the cookies in twos, separated by parchment paper, back-to-back in cellophane bags and then tie with a ribbon or twist tie. They will keep for up to 1 week. **MAKES ABOUT 3 DOZEN COOKIES**

1¼ cup all-purpose flour

¾ teaspoon baking soda

½ teaspoon baking powder

¼ teaspoon salt

1 cup (2 sticks) unsalted butter, at room temperature

½ cup granulated sugar

½ cup lightly packed brown sugar

½ cup creamy peanut butter

1 large egg, at room temperature

¼ teaspoon pure vanilla extract

½ cup crushed lightly salted peanuts

¼ cup fruit preserves of your choice

1. In a medium-size bowl, combine the flour, baking soda, baking powder, and salt.

2. In the bowl of an electric mixer, beat the butter and both sugars on medium speed until light and fluffy. Add the peanut butter, egg, and vanilla; mix again until blended, scraping down the sides of the bowl if necessary. Add the flour mixture and mix on low speed until incorporated. Fold in the peanuts. Refrigerate the dough for 30 minutes.

3. Preheat the oven to 350°F. Line two baking sheets with parchment paper or silicone baking liners; set aside.

4. With your hands or a cookie dough scoop, shape the dough into 1-inch balls. Place the dough balls on the prepared baking sheets, about 2 inches apart, and flatten them slightly with your hands. With your fingertip, create an indentation in the center of each cookie and fill each with ¼ teaspoon preserves. Bake until the edges are lightly browned, 10 to 12 minutes.

5. Cool the cookies on the pans for 5 minutes before transferring them to a rack to cool completely. Repeat with the remaining dough. Pack in zipper-top plastic bags, pressing out any air, or in airtight containers, separating the layers with waxed or parchment paper. Alternatively, stack in cellophane bags and secure with string or ribbon.

Vanilla Bean Sugar Cookies

One of the most expensive spices, vanilla pods (or fruit) come from the orchid plant. You can scrape the oily seeds from the inside of the pods and add them to baked goods to give an intense vanilla aroma and speckled appearance. Save the leftover pods to make vanilla sugar (just add the pods to a container of granulated sugar). These cookies will keep for up to 1 week. **MAKES ABOUT 5 DOZEN COOKIES**

2¾ cups all-purpose flour

3 teaspoons baking powder

¼ teaspoon salt

1 cup (2 sticks) unsalted butter, at room temperature

1½ cups sugar

½ vanilla bean

2 large eggs, at room temperature

¼ cup colored or white sparkling sugar (optional)

Oven Check

The correct oven temperature is essential when baking. If you think your oven temperature may be off, buy an oven thermometer from the hardware store or department store so that you can calculate the difference appropriately when baking.

1. Preheat the oven to 350°F. Line two baking sheets with parchment paper or silicone baking liners; set aside.

2. In a medium-size bowl, combine the flour, baking powder, and salt.

3. In the bowl of an electric mixer, beat the butter and sugar on medium speed until light and fluffy. With a sharp knife, split the vanilla bean and scrape the seeds out of the pod. Add the seeds and eggs to the butter mixture and mix until blended. Add the flour mixture and mix on low speed until blended.

4. With your hands or a cookie dough scoop, form 1-inch balls with the cookie dough. Place the dough balls on the prepared baking sheets, about 2 inches apart. Bake until the edges begin to brown, 9 to 10 minutes. (Once the cookies have spread, after about 5 minutes, sprinkle some sparkling sugar on top of the cookies, if desired.)

5. Cool the cookies on the baking sheets for 5 minutes before transferring to a rack to cool completely. Repeat with the remaining dough. Pack in zipper-top plastic bags, pressing out any air, or in airtight containers, separating the layers with waxed or parchment paper. Alternatively, pack a handful together in cellophane bags tied closed with ribbon.

Chewy Oatmeal-Raisin Cookies

Soaking the raisins beforehand helps increase the moisture content of these classic cookies, preventing them from drying out over time. For additional flavor, try soaking the raisins in orange juice or dark rum instead of water. Ship them to a nearby loved one, as they will keep for up to 1 week. **MAKES ABOUT 2 DOZEN COOKIES**

1. Put the raisins in a small bowl and cover with boiling water. Let the raisins soak for 5 minutes, then drain.

2. In a medium-size bowl, combine the flour, baking soda, cinnamon, nutmeg, and salt.

3. In the bowl of an electric mixer, beat the butter and brown sugar on medium speed until light and fluffy. Add the egg and vanilla, and mix again to combine, scraping the sides of the bowl if necessary. Add the flour mixture and mix on low speed until just combined. Fold in the oats and raisins. Refrigerate the mixture for at least 1 hour.

4. Preheat the oven to 350°F. Line two baking sheets with parchment paper or silicone baking liners.

5. Using your hands or a cookie dough scoop, form 1-inch balls with the dough. Place the dough balls on the prepared baking sheets, about 2 inches apart. Bake until the edges begin to brown, 7 to 8 minutes.

6. Cool the cookies on the pans for 5 minutes before transferring to a rack to cool completely. Pack in zipper-top plastic bags, pressing out any air, or in airtight containers, separating the layers with waxed or parchment paper.

½ cup raisins

¾ cup all-purpose flour

½ teaspoon baking soda

½ teaspoon ground cinnamon

⅛ teaspoon ground nutmeg or allspice

¼ teaspoon salt

8 tablespoons (1 stick) unsalted butter, melted

¾ cup packed light or dark brown sugar

1 large egg, at room temperature

½ teaspoon pure vanilla extract

1½ cups old-fashioned rolled oats

Herbes de Provence Cornmeal Cookies

Herbes de Provence is a blend of dried herbs commonly found in the south of France. The mix varies depending on the producer, but it generally contains thyme, rosemary, savory, lavender, marjoram, basil, and sage. You can find the blend in most supermarkets or gourmet shops. These will keep for up to 10 days. **MAKES 7 TO 8 DOZEN COOKIES**

1. In a medium size bowl, combine the flour, cornmeal, salt, and herbes de Provence.

2. In the bowl of an electric mixer, beat the butter and sugar on medium speed until light and fluffy. Add the vanilla and lemon zest and mix for another minute or two. Gradually add the flour mixture and mix until combined. Divide the dough in half and transfer the dough to pieces of waxed or parchment paper. Shape the dough into two square logs, each about 12 inches long and 1½ inches in diameter, and wrap the paper around the dough. Refrigerate until the dough is stiff, about an hour.

3. Preheat the oven to 350°F. Line two baking sheets with parchment paper or silicone baking liners.

4. Remove the dough logs from the refrigerator. Sprinkle sparkling sugar on the work surface. Roll the logs in the sugar to coat the outsides. Slice the dough into ¼-inch-thick pieces. Place the pieces on the prepared baking sheets, about 1 inch apart. Bake until the edges of the cookies look lightly browned, 12 to 15 minutes.

5. Allow the cookies to completely cool on the baking sheets. Repeat with the remaining dough. Pack in zipper-top plastic bags, pressing out any air, or in airtight containers, separating the layers with waxed or parchment paper. Take care to fill empty spaces with crumpled paper for extra cushioning.

2 cups all-purpose flour

¼ cup yellow cornmeal

1 teaspoon kosher salt

1 teaspoon dried herbes de Provence

1 cup (2 sticks) unsalted butter, softened

¾ cup confectioners' sugar

2 teaspoons pure vanilla extract

1 tablespoon freshly grated lemon zest

Sparkling sugar

Kitchen Sink Cookies

The glory of these cookies is that you can add whatever ingredients you like to the basic cookie dough. Most of the time (cross your fingers!) they'll turn out delicious, so feel free to add whatever you can find in the kitchen. For care packages, I like to include them in a selection with chocolate chip and oatmeal-raisin cookies for variety. They will keep for up to 1 week. **MAKES ABOUT 4 DOZEN COOKIES**

2 cups all-purpose flour

½ teaspoon baking soda

½ teaspoon salt

12 tablespoons (1½ sticks) unsalted butter, melted

1 cup packed light brown sugar

¼ cup granulated sugar

1 large egg, at room temperature

1 large egg yolk, at room temperature

1 teaspoon pure vanilla extract

½ cup semisweet chocolate chips

1 cup old-fashioned rolled oats, crushed potato chips, pretzels, raisins, nuts, or unsweetened shredded coconut, or any combination

1. Preheat the oven to 350°F. Line two baking sheets with parchment paper or silicone baking liners; set aside.

2. In a medium-size bowl, whisk together the flour, baking soda, and salt.

3. In the bowl of an electric mixer, beat the butter and both sugars on medium speed until light and fluffy. Add the egg, egg yolk, and vanilla, and mix until well combined, scraping down the sides of the bowl if necessary. Add the flour mixture and mix on low speed until blended. Fold in the chocolate chips and oats or other ingredients of your choice. (If time permits, refrigerating the dough for at least 12 hours before baking will improve the flavor of these cookies.)

4. Using your hands or a cookie dough scoop, form 1-inch balls with the dough. Place the dough balls on the prepared baking sheets, about 2 inches apart. Bake until the edges are lightly browned, 9 to 10 minutes. They will look slightly underdone in the center.

5. Cool the cookies on the pans for 5 minutes before transferring to a rack to cool completely. Repeat with the remaining dough. Pack in zipper-top plastic bags, pressing out any air, or in airtight containers, separating the layers with waxed or parchment paper.

Chocolate *and* Orange Marmalade Oat Cookies

While they sound fancy, these are modest oat cookies gussied up with semisweet chocolate chips and sweet orange marmalade. Make them when you want to create a classy package for your favorite gourmand, or send them to any friend who likes the finer things in life. These will keep for 5 days. **MAKES ABOUT 4 DOZEN COOKIES**

1. Preheat the oven to 350°F. Line two baking sheets with parchment paper or silicone baking liners; set aside.

2. In a medium-size bowl, combine the flour, oats, baking powder, cinnamon, and salt.

3. In the bowl of an electric mixer, beat the butter, sugar, and marmalade on medium speed until well combined. Add the egg and vanilla, and mix again for another minute or two, scraping down the sides of the bowl if necessary. Add the flour mixture and mix on low speed until combined. Fold in the chocolate chips. Using your hands or a cookie dough scoop, form 1-inch balls with the dough. Place the dough balls on the prepared baking sheets, about 2 inches apart. Bake until the edges begin to brown, 9 to 10 minutes.

4. Let the cookies cool on the baking sheets for 10 minutes before transferring to a rack to cool completely. Repeat with the remaining dough. Pack in zipper-top plastic bags, pressing out any air, or in airtight containers, separating the layers with waxed or parchment paper.

2¼ cups all-purpose flour

¾ cup old-fashioned rolled oats

1½ teaspoons baking powder

1 teaspoon ground cinnamon

1 teaspoon salt

8 tablespoons (1 stick) unsalted butter, at room temperature

½ cup sugar

½ cup orange marmalade

1 large egg, at room temperature

1 teaspoon pure vanilla extract

½ cup semisweet chocolate chips

Chocolate-Cherry Ranger Cookies

Depending on which story you believe, the original name for these cookies was either "Texas Ranger Cookies" or "Lone Ranger Cookies." Regardless, these high-energy cookies are rich and satisfying and have a 1-week shelf life. While they typically contain oats, coconut, and cereal to give them some crunch, I've added dried cherries and chocolate for extra flavor and texture. MAKES ABOUT 5 DOZEN COOKIES

2 cups all-purpose flour

1 cup old-fashioned rolled oats

1 cup unsweetened shredded coconut

1 teaspoon baking soda

1 teaspoon salt

½ teaspoon baking powder

1 cup (2 sticks) unsalted butter, at room temperature

1 cup packed light brown sugar

1 cup granulated sugar

2 large eggs, at room temperature

1 teaspoon pure vanilla extract

⅔ cup semisweet chocolate chips

⅔ cup dried cherries

1. Preheat the oven to 350°F. Line two baking sheets with parchment paper or silicone baking liners; set aside.

2. In a medium-size bowl, combine the flour, oats, coconut, baking soda, salt, and baking powder.

3. In the bowl of an electric mixer, mix the butter and both sugars on medium speed until light and fluffy. Add the eggs and vanilla, and mix until combined. Gradually add the flour mixture and mix until just combined. Fold in the chocolate chips and cherries.

4. Using your hands or a cookie dough scoop, shape the dough into 1-inch balls. Place the dough balls on the prepared baking sheets, about 2 inches apart. Bake until the cookies are golden brown, 9 to 11 minutes.

5. Let the cookies cool for 5 minutes on the baking sheet before transferring them to a rack to cool completely. Repeat with the remaining dough. Pack in zipper-top plastic bags, pressing out any air, or in airtight containers, separating the layers with waxed or parchment paper. Alternatively, stack the cookies in cellophane bags. Tie the tops of the bags together with string or ribbon.

Freezing Cookies

If you're making cookies ahead of time, you can freeze them for at least 6 months. Freeze in a single layer and then store them layered in an airtight freezer-safe container. Label and date the containers so you don't forget what's what! Thaw cookies at room temperature for 30 minutes.

Chocolate-Peanut Butter Chip Cookies

The small amount of espresso powder in these cookies enhances their rich, dark cocoa flavor. Send them to the chocolate and peanut butter lover in your life or to someone who just needs a little sweet pick-me-up during the week. Ship them fast, though—these will keep for 5 days. **MAKES ABOUT 3 DOZEN COOKIES**

1 cup all-purpose flour

¼ cup plus 2 tablespoons Dutch-processed cocoa powder, sifted

½ teaspoon baking soda

¼ teaspoon salt

12 tablespoons (1½ sticks) unsalted butter, at room temperature

⅔ cup sugar

¼ teaspoon instant espresso powder or coffee granules

1 large egg, at room temperature

1 teaspoon pure vanilla extract

1 cup peanut butter chips

1. In a medium-size bowl, combine the flour, cocoa powder, baking soda, and salt.

2. In the bowl of an electric mixer, beat the butter, sugar, and espresso powder on medium speed until light and fluffy. Add the egg and vanilla, and mix until combined. Add the flour mixture and mix on low speed until incorporated. Fold in the peanut butter chips. Refrigerate the dough for at least 1 hour.

3. Preheat the oven to 350°F. Line two baking sheets with parchment paper or silicone baking liners; set aside.

4. With your hands or a cookie dough scoop, shape the dough into 1-inch balls. Place the dough balls on the prepared baking sheets, about 2 inches apart. Bake until the edges are firm to the touch, 9 to 10 minutes.

5. Cool the cookies completely on the baking sheets. Repeat with the remaining dough. Pack in zipper-top plastic bags, pressing out any air, or in airtight containers, separating the layers with waxed or parchment paper.

Glazed Coconut-Lime Shortbread

A tropical variation on a classic cookie, these treats are brightened up with the addition of chewy coconut and tart lime zest and juice. Make sure that the glaze is completely set before packaging the shortbread so that it does not smear and rub off during shipping. These treats are perfect for long-distance travel, as they keep for about 2 weeks. **MAKES 16 COOKIES**

1. Preheat the oven to 350°F. Line an 8-inch square pan with parchment paper, leaving extra for overhang; set aside.

2. Make the shortbread: In a medium-size bowl, combine the flour, coconut, and salt.

3. In the bowl of an electric mixer, beat the butter and granulated sugar on medium speed until light and fluffy. Add the vanilla and lime zest; mix until combined. Add the flour mixture and mix on low speed until combined. Transfer the mixture to the prepared pan and firmly press into the bottom of the pan. Bake until the edges of the shortbread are golden, 30 to 35 minutes. Let the shortbread cool in the pan.

4. Meanwhile, make the glaze: In a small bowl, mix the confectioners' sugar, lime juice, and zest together until well combined.

5. Remove the shortbread from the pan by grasping the ends of the parchment paper. Slice into 16 squares and place on a rack. Drizzle the glaze over the bars and let set completely.

6. Wrap each bar individually with plastic wrap or waxed or parchment paper, seal with tape, and place in a zipper-top plastic bag. Alternatively, layer the bars in airtight containers (preferably square or rectangular), separating the layers with waxed or parchment paper, and filling the empty spaces with crumpled waxed or parchment paper.

SHORTBREAD

2¼ cups all-purpose flour

1 cup sweetened shredded coconut

¼ teaspoon salt

1 cup (2 sticks) unsalted butter, at room temperature

⅓ cup granulated sugar

½ teaspoon pure vanilla extract

1 heaping tablespoon freshly grated lime zest

GLAZE

1 cup confectioners' sugar

2 tablespoons freshly squeezed lime juice

1 teaspoon freshly grated lime zest

ANZAC Biscuits

Originally called "soldier's biscuits," these oat-based cookies were first developed during World War I as a cheap and nonperishable treat for members of the Australian and New Zealand Army Corps. Many army wives and families used to ship the cookies to their loved ones because they were easy to make and had a long shelf life. The classic recipe includes golden syrup, but I have adapted this recipe with honey. Feel free to dress up the cookie with nuts and chopped dried fruit, if you like. They are sturdy and keep for up to 2 weeks, making them a perfect candidate for the soldier in your life. **MAKES ABOUT 2 DOZEN COOKIES**

1. Preheat the oven to 350°F. Line two baking sheets with parchment paper or silicone baking liners; set aside.

2. In a medium-size bowl, combine the flour, oats, coconut, and both sugars.

3. In a 2-quart saucepan over medium heat, melt the butter and honey, stirring until combined. While the butter and honey are melting, in a small bowl stir the boiling water and baking soda together and then stir into the butter and honey mixture. The mixture will bubble. Pour the mixture over the flour mixture and stir to combine.

4. Using your hands or a cookie dough scoop, form 1-inch balls with the dough. Place the dough balls on the prepared baking sheets, about 2 inches apart, and press the dough down to flatten. Bake until the cookies are golden brown, 10 to 12 minutes.

5. Cool the cookies on the baking sheets for 5 minutes before transferring to a rack to cool completely. For that old-fashioned appeal, pack the cookies in food-safe cookie tins, separated by layers of waxed or parchment paper. Alternatively, you may package them loosely in zipper-top plastic bags, pressing out any air.

1 cup all-purpose flour

1 cup old-fashioned rolled oats

½ cup unsweetened shredded coconut

⅓ cup granulated sugar

⅓ cup packed light brown sugar

8 tablespoons (1 stick) unsalted butter

1 tablespoon honey or light corn syrup

2 tablespoons boiling water

1 teaspoon baking soda

Raspberry-Lemon Linzer Cookies

Use good-quality raspberry preserves for the filling. I prefer the kind with the seeds because it seems to have a more even consistency and spreads well. The warmed preserves may seem runny at first, but they will thicken and become stickier when cooled. These cookies keep for about 1 week, though they will soften slightly during shipping. **MAKES ABOUT 3 DOZEN COOKIES**

½ cup toasted whole almonds (see page 95)

½ cup packed light brown sugar

2½ cups all-purpose flour, plus more for rolling

½ teaspoon baking powder

½ teaspoon salt

1 cup (2 sticks) unsalted butter

1 large egg, at room temperature

1 teaspoon pure vanilla extract

1½ tablespoons freshly grated lemon zest

1 cup raspberry jam

1. In the bowl of a food processor, process the almonds and brown sugar until the nuts are finely ground. Add the flour, baking powder, and salt. Pulse several times until the mixture is combined.

2. In the bowl of an electric mixer, beat the butter, egg, vanilla, and lemon zest on medium speed until light and fluffy. Add the flour mixture and mix on low speed until blended. Divide the dough in half and form into two disks. Wrap each disk in plastic wrap and refrigerate for at least 2 hours.

3. Preheat the oven to 350°F. Line two baking sheets with parchment paper or silicone baking liners.

4. Place each dough disk on a floured surface. Using a rolling pin, roll the dough to a ⅛-inch thickness. Using a 2-inch round cookie cutter, cut out cookies. Reroll the dough scraps and cut out more cookies. Place the cookies on the prepared baking sheets, about 1 inch apart. Bake until the edges are golden brown, 9 to 10 minutes.

5. Cool the cookies on the baking sheets for 5 minutes before transferring to a rack to cool completely. Repeat with the remaining dough.

6. In a small saucepan, warm the jam over low heat. Use a fine-mesh strainer to strain out the seeds, if desired. Spread about 1 teaspoon of preserves on the underside of half of the cookies and then top with another cookie to make a sandwich. Cool the cookies on cooling racks. Pack in airtight containers, separating the layers with waxed or parchment paper.

Chocolate-Caramel Surprise Cookies

While they may look like ordinary chocolate cookies, these treats have a little surprise inside. I experimented with a bunch of different candies for this cookie and settled on foil-wrapped chocolate caramels because they retained a good consistency after baking and were not too soft. The candies also keep the cookies moist and chewy for 5 days after baking. **MAKES ABOUT 5 DOZEN COOKIES**

1. In a medium-size bowl, combine the flour, cocoa powder, baking soda, and salt.

2. In the bowl of an electric mixer, beat the butter and both sugars on medium speed until light and fluffy. Add the eggs and vanilla, and mix until combined. Add the flour mixture and mix on low speed until incorporated. Refrigerate the dough for at least 1 hour.

3. Preheat the oven to 350°F. Line two baking sheets with parchment paper or silicone baking liners. Unwrap the candies.

4. Taking a small amount of cookie dough (about 2 teaspoons), stuff the caramel candy into the dough and roll the dough around it, making a ball. Make sure that the candy is not exposed or else it will not stay inside the cookie. Place the balls on the prepared baking sheets, about 2 inches apart. Bake until the cookies have firm edges but soft centers, 9 to 10 minutes.

5. Cool the cookies completely on the baking sheets. Repeat with the remaining dough. Pack in zipper-top plastic bags, pressing out any air, or in airtight containers, separating the layers with waxed or parchment paper.

2¼ cups all-purpose flour

1 cup natural unsweetened cocoa powder, sifted

1 teaspoon baking soda

½ teaspoon salt

1 cup (2 sticks) unsalted butter, at room temperature

1 cup granulated sugar

1 cup packed light brown sugar

2 large eggs, at room temperature

1 teaspoon pure vanilla extract

1 (12-ounce) package chocolate-covered caramel candies (such as Rolos)

Almond-Pistachio Chewies

Similar to Italian pignoli cookies, these chewy treats have a bright and refreshing flavor from the lemon zest and a crunch from the crushed pistachios. They are great for shipping long distances because they are sturdy and keep for more than 2 weeks, actually improving in flavor over that time. The secret is the almond paste, which helps the cookies stay moist and flavorful. **MAKES ABOUT 4 DOZEN COOKIES**

1. Preheat the oven to 325°F. Line two baking sheets with parchment paper or silicone baking liners; set aside.

2. In the bowl of an electric mixer, mix the almond paste on low speed to soften. Add the egg whites and mix on medium speed until fully incorporated. Add the sugar, honey, lemon zest, and salt, and mix on low speed.

3. Scatter the pistachios on a plate. Using your hands or a cookie dough scoop, form 1-inch balls with the dough. Coat one side of each dough ball with the nuts and transfer them to the prepared baking sheets with the nuts facing up, about 1 inch apart. Bake until the cookies are light golden brown, 20 to 22 minutes.

4. Cool the cookies on the baking sheets for 10 minutes before transferring to a rack to cool completely. Repeat with the remaining dough. Pack the cookies in a round airtight container, separating the layers with waxed or parchment paper. Alternatively, stack the cookies in cellophane bags. Tie the tops of the bags together with string or ribbon.

2 (8-ounce) cans almond paste (not marzipan), broken into pieces

2 large egg whites, at room temperature

1⅓ cups confectioners' sugar

2 tablespoons honey

2 teaspoons freshly grated lemon zest

½ teaspoon salt

⅔ cup crushed pistachios

Scoop It Up

Ever wonder how bakeries get such evenly sized cookies? It's not that they have magical hands or super-special ovens; they use scoops. If you use a scoop to portion out cookie dough, the cookies will be very close to the same size. Experiment with different sizes to create your own monster pucks or dainty two-bite wonders. Keep in mind that different-size scoops may require different baking times for cookies.

Lemon-Cardamom Meltaways

These melt-in-your-mouth cookies get their pungent and warm flavor from cardamom. You can buy cardamom as whole pods or already ground. I prefer grinding the
seeds myself in a mortar and pestle because they have a more intense flavor, but
preground is fine, too. These keep for up to 2 weeks. **MAKES ABOUT 8 DOZEN COOKIES**

Scant 2 cups all-purpose
flour

2 tablespoons cornstarch

¼ teaspoon kosher salt

½ teaspoon ground
cardamom

12 tablespoons (1½ sticks)
unsalted butter, at room
temperature

1 cup confectioners' sugar

¼ cup freshly grated lemon
zest

2 tablespoons freshly
squeezed lemon juice

2 teaspoons pure vanilla
extract

Cookie Check

Check your cookies a
few minutes before the
recommended baking
time given in the reci-
pes to avoid overcook-
ing. Some cookies may
bake a little faster or
slower, depending on
oven temperature or
the weather.

1. In a medium-size bowl, combine the flour, cornstarch, salt, and
cardamom.

2. In the bowl of an electric mixer, beat the butter and ⅓ cup of the sugar
on medium speed until light and fluffy. Add the lemon zest, juice, and
vanilla, and mix on low speed until combined. Divide the dough in half
and transfer to pieces of waxed or parchment paper. Shape the dough
into two square logs, each about 12 inches long and 1 inch in diameter,
and wrap the paper around the dough. Refrigerate until the dough is stiff,
about an hour.

3. Preheat the oven to 350°F. Line two baking sheets with parchment
paper or silicone baking liners. Place the remaining ⅔ cup sugar on a plate
or in a zipper-top plastic bag.

4. Remove the dough from the refrigerator and slice each log into
¼-inch-thick pieces. Place the pieces on the prepared baking sheets,
about 1 inch apart, and bake until golden, 12 to 15 minutes.

5. Allow to cookies to begin cooling on the baking sheets for 5 minutes.
While the cookies are still warm, dredge them in the sugar. Shake off the
excess sugar and place on a rack to cool completely. Repeat with the
remaining dough. Pack in zipper-top plastic bags, pressing out any air,
or in airtight containers, separating the layers with waxed or parchment
paper. Alternatively, stack them in small cellophane bags secured with
ribbon.

Chinese Almond Cookies

During high school, my sister and I spent our summers working in our parents' Chinese restaurant, called Hunan, in Manchester, New Hampshire. Of the two dessert dishes we served, I was fond of the giant almond cookies that nobody could get through in one sitting. I re-created those crisp and crumbly cookies in this recipe, except I made them more reasonably sized. I occasionally ship them to my sister as a reminder of our teenage days. They will keep for up to 1 week. **MAKES ABOUT 4 DOZEN COOKIES**

1. Preheat the oven to 325°F. Line two baking sheets with parchment paper or silicone baking liners; set aside.

2. In a medium-size bowl, combine the flour, baking soda, and salt.

3. In the bowl of an electric mixer, beat the butter, shortening, and sugar on medium speed until light and fluffy. Add the egg, both extracts, and yellow food coloring (if using); mix again. Add the flour mixture and mix on low speed until the dough is dry and crumbly. Using your hands or a cookie dough scoop, form 1-inch balls with the dough. Place the dough balls on the prepared baking sheets, about 2 inches apart. Place an almond on top of each cookie ball and press down with the palms of your hands to embed the almond and flatten the cookie.

4. In a small bowl, break up the egg yolks with a fork. Brush the tops of the cookies with the yolk. Bake until the tops of the cookies are crackled and golden brown, 15 to 18 minutes.

5. Cool the cookies on the baking sheets for 5 minutes before transferring to a rack to cool completely. Repeat with the remaining dough. Wrap the cookies individually with plastic wrap or parchment or waxed paper, seal with tape, and then pack them in Chinese takeout containers or food-safe tins.

2¾ cups all-purpose flour

1 teaspoon baking soda

½ teaspoon salt

8 tablespoons (1 stick) unsalted butter, at room temperature

¼ cup vegetable shortening

1 cup sugar

1 large egg, at room temperature

1 teaspoon pure almond extract

½ teaspoon pure vanilla extract

2 to 3 drops yellow food coloring (optional)

½ cup blanched whole almonds

2 large egg yolks, at room temperature

Tricolored Peppermint-Striped Cookies

Holiday pinwheel cookies look stunning, but they may be frustrating to make. Here's an easy variation that only requires you to stack different color doughs and then roll. They look just as interesting, are fun to eat, and keep for up to 10 days, making them perfect for shipping to Aunt Clara across the country. **MAKES ABOUT 12 DOZEN COOKIES**

4 cups all-purpose flour, plus more for rolling

1 teaspoon baking powder

¼ teaspoon baking soda

1 teaspoon salt

1 cup (2 sticks) plus 5 tablespoons unsalted butter, at room temperature

1⅔ cup sugar

2 large eggs, at room temperature

1 teaspoon peppermint extract

2 to 3 drops red food coloring

1 teaspoon pure vanilla extract

2 teaspoons natural unsweetened cocoa powder, sifted

1. In a medium-size bowl, combine the flour, baking powder, baking soda, and salt.

2. In the bowl of an electric mixer, beat the butter and sugar on medium speed until light and fluffy. Add the eggs, and mix for another minute or two, scraping down the sides of the bowl if necessary. Add the flour mixture and mix again until blended.

3. Divide the dough into thirds and place each portion in a separate bowl. Mix the peppermint extract and a few drops of the red food coloring into the dough in one bowl. Add ½ teaspoon of the vanilla to the dough in each of the remaining two bowls and mix until blended. Mix the cocoa powder into one of the vanilla-flavored doughs. In the end, you should have three doughs: one red, one white, and one brown. Wrap all three doughs separately in plastic wrap and refrigerate for at least 1 hour.

4. Preheat the oven to 375°F. Line two baking sheets with parchment paper or silicone baking liners; set aside.

5. Remove the doughs from the refrigerator and divide each color dough in half. Using a rolling pin, roll each of the six dough sections into a circle 8 to 9 inches in diameter and ¼ inch thick, using extra flour if necessary to keep the dough from sticking. Start with one chocolate layer on the bottom, and stack one each of the vanilla dough and then the peppermint dough on top. Repeat with the other three circles to make a separate stack. Refrigerate the two layered stacks for 15 minutes.

6. Roll each layered dough stacked to a ¼-inch thickness, pressing the three colors together. Using a 1½-inch round cookie cutter, cut out the cookies as close together as possible. Discard the scraps. Place the cookies on the prepared baking sheets, about 1 inch apart. Bake until the edges begin to brown, 6 to 7 minutes.

7. Cool the cookies on the baking sheets for 5 minutes before transferring to a rack to cool completely. Repeat with the remaining dough. Stack the cookies in cellophane bags and tie with a festive ribbon.

Care Package CPR

If you are concerned that your cookies might be dead on arrival, include a note to your recipient on how to revive them: Put a slice or two of bread in the bag or tin with the cookies. The bread will release moisture that the cookies will absorb, making them soft again. This technique works with stale marshmallows too.

Dirty Snowballs

I love snow, especially when it coats tree branches and buildings and illuminates my neighborhood with a warm, white glow. However, when you live in an urban area, as I do, the snow quickly attracts dirt and turns an unsightly gray (or even yellow)! Inspired by this urban snowscape, I created a chocolate-flavored macaroon that is much more appetizing than a dirty snowball. If you have a friend who loves coconut or perhaps appreciates a tongue-in-cheek kind of treat, ship these to him or her. They'll keep for 1 week. **MAKES ABOUT 3 DOZEN MACAROONS**

1 (14-ounce) can sweetened condensed milk

¼ cup natural unsweetened cocoa powder

5¼ to 5½ cups unsweetened shredded coconut

1. Preheat the oven to 350°F. Line two baking sheets with parchment paper or silicone baking liners; set aside.

2. Put the condensed milk and cocoa powder in a medium-size bowl. Using a spatula, stir the mixture until the cocoa is well incorporated into the milk. Add the coconut, and blend to lightly coat the flakes with the milk mixture. The mixture should not be very wet, so adjust the amount of coconut accordingly.

3. Spoon tablespoons of the mixture onto the prepared sheets and bake until the tops of the cookies are lightly browned, 10 to 12 minutes.

4. Cool for 5 minutes on the baking sheets before transferring to a rack to cool completely. Repeat with the remaining dough. Stack the macaroons in cellophane bags and secure the bags with ribbon or raffia.

Sweetened vs. Unsweetened Coconut

To cut down on the sweetness, I've used unsweetened shredded coconut. You can usually find this in the supermarket baking aisle or at health food stores.

Chocolate-Hazelnut Biscotti

The perfect accompaniment to a cup of coffee or tea, biscotti (meaning "twice cooked" in Italian) are well known for their distinctive shape and crisp, dry texture. These dunkable cookies, which date back hundreds of years, have a long shelf life. Traditionally, biscotti do not contain butter or oil, but I added a little bit of butter to this version to make the cookie tender yet still crisp. This does shorten their lifespan a bit, but nonetheless these will keep for 2 weeks. **MAKES ABOUT 4 DOZEN BISCOTTI**

1. Preheat the oven to 350°F. Line two baking sheets with parchment paper or silicone baking liners; set aside.

2. In a medium-size bowl, combine the flour, cocoa, baking soda, and salt.

3. In the bowl of an electric mixer, beat the butter and sugar on medium speed until light and fluffy. Add the eggs one at a time, mixing to incorporate after each one. Add the vanilla and mix for another minute. Add the flour mixture and mix until fully incorporated. Fold in the hazelnuts. Divide the dough in half and transfer each half to a prepared baking sheet. Using floured hands, shape the dough into two loaves, each about 12 inches in length and 1 inch tall. Bake for 30 minutes.

4. Remove the baking sheets from the oven and let the logs cool for 15 to 20 minutes. Using a serrated knife, slice the logs into ½-inch-thick pieces. Place the biscotti on their cut sides on the baking sheets and bake for another 15 minutes, turning them over halfway through.

5. Transfer the biscotti to a rack and let them cool completely. Pack in zipper-top plastic bags, pressing out any air, or in airtight containers. Alternatively, stack the biscotti in cellophane bags secured with a ribbon.

2 cups all-purpose flour

⅔ cup Dutch-processed cocoa powder, sifted

1 teaspoon baking soda

½ teaspoon salt

6 tablespoons (¾ stick) unsalted butter, at room temperature

1 cup sugar

2 large eggs, at room temperature

2 teaspoons pure vanilla extract

1 cup toasted hazelnuts, chopped (see page 95)

Cornmeal-Blueberry Biscotti

These rustic cookies are crisp and chewy and can handle the tough conditions of shipping. They also keep for up to 2 weeks, making them ideal for shipping across the country or around the globe to your loved ones. **MAKES ABOUT 2 DOZEN BISCOTTI**

1. Preheat the oven to 350°F. Line two baking sheets with parchment paper or silicone baking liners; set aside.

2. In a medium-size bowl, combine the flour, cornmeal, baking soda, and salt.

3. In the bowl of an electric mixer, beat the butter and sugar on medium speed until light and fluffy. Add the eggs and mix until combined, scraping down the sides of the bowl if necessary. Add the flour mixture and mix on low speed until blended. Fold in the blueberries. Place the dough on one of the prepared baking sheets. Using floured hands, pat the dough into a log, about 12 inches long and 1 inch tall. Bake until the edges of the dough look dry and light brown, 20 to 30 minutes. The dough will spread and double its original size.

4. Let the log cool on the baking sheet for 30 minutes. Turn down the heat of the oven to 250°F.

5. Using a serrated knife, slice the log into ½-inch-thick pieces. Place the biscotti on their cut sides on the baking sheets and return to the oven for another 40 to 60 minutes, or until the biscotti are dry. Turn the biscotti over and bake for another 5 minutes.

6. Transfer the biscotti to a rack and let them cool completely. Pack in zipper-top plastic bags, pressing out any air, or in airtight containers, separating the layers with waxed or parchment paper.

1 cup all-purpose flour

½ cup fine- or medium-ground cornmeal

1 teaspoon baking soda

Pinch of salt

4 tablespoons (½ stick) unsalted butter, at room temperature

½ cup sugar

2 large eggs, at room temperature

⅔ cup dried blueberries

Chewy Mocha Caramels 86

Chocolate-Almond Toffee 87

Peppermint Fantasy Fudge 88

Happy Hours 90

Honey Granola Bars 91

Whole-Wheat Almond and Orange Biscotti 92

Brown Sugar Crisps 93

Green Tea Shortbread Bites 94

Salted Nut Brittle 95

Cherry, Hazelnut, and Pistachio Nougat 96

Spiced Cocoa-Dusted Nuts 98

Chocolate-Ginger Rum Balls 99

Cinnamon-Spice Popcorn 100

Caramel-Pecan Popcorn Balls 101

Cinnamon Marshmallows 102

No-Bake Swedish Coco Balls 103

CONFECTIONS that go THE EXTRA MILE

Shipping a package around the world? You'll want dependable and reliable treats that can take the extra mileage and last through rough rides and long road trips—just like a good car! In this chapter, I've assembled some of my favorite recipes that last for extended periods of time without showing signs of age. When packing these confections, avoid combining different treats in the same container or plastic bag; give each an individual container. Otherwise the different textures, flavors, and moisture contents may interfere with each other.

Chewy Mocha Caramels

As a coffee lover, I'm always trying to find a way to incorporate the deep aromatic flavor of coffee and espresso into my desserts. In this recipe, instant espresso powder and cocoa powder give the candies just enough bitterness to temper the sweetness of the sugar and complement the richness of the caramel. Long lasting, these treats keep for about 1 month and are ideal for college students, those in the Armed Forces, and just about anybody who needs a sweet jolt. Pack them in Mason jars, old coffee cans, or decorative containers and bags to make them extra special. **MAKES 6 TO 7 DOZEN CARAMELS**

1 cup plus 2 tablespoons heavy cream

5 tablespoons unsalted butter

2 tablespoons instant espresso powder or coffee granules

4 teaspoons natural unsweetened cocoa powder

½ teaspoon kosher salt

1½ cups sugar

¼ cup light corn syrup

¼ cup water

1. Line an 8-inch square pan with parchment paper, leaving extra for overhang; set aside.

2. In a small saucepan over low heat, combine the heavy cream, butter, espresso powder, cocoa, and salt. Heat until the mixture is warm and combined, whisking constantly.

3. In a large heavy-bottomed saucepan fitted with a candy thermometer, combine the sugar, corn syrup, and water. Bring the mixture to a boil over medium-high heat and cook, stirring occasionally, until the mixture turns golden, 10 to 12 minutes. Carefully add the cream mixture to the pan—it will bubble violently, so use caution. Bring the mixture up to 245°F. Quickly pour the caramel into the prepared pan and allow the mixture to cool at room temperature until set, about 2 hours.

4. Grasping the parchment paper, remove the caramel from the pan and place on a cutting board. Using a sharp knife, cut the caramels into small bite-size pieces. Wrap in candy wrappers, waxed paper, or parchment paper and pack the candies in zipper-top plastic bags or airtight containers.

Chocolate-Almond Toffee

Toffee is a great option for shipping because of its hard texture and natural "broken" appearance. While the chocolate on top of this version can make the treat a bit unstable, I suggest tempering the chocolate to raise its melting temperature and help keep its glossy appearance. This treat is best when shipped in moderate temperatures and will keep for up to a month, or even longer. **MAKES ABOUT 1¼ POUNDS TOFFEE**

1. Line a sheet pan with parchment paper or a silicone baking liner; set aside.

2. In a heavy-bottomed 2-quart saucepan with a candy thermometer attached, combine the brown sugar, butter, water, and corn syrup. Dissolve the ingredients over medium heat, occasionally swirling the pot. Bring the mixture up to 285°F. The mixture will be bubbly. Remove the pot from the heat and stir in the vanilla and baking soda. The mixture will slightly increase in volume. Pour the toffee onto the prepared pan and let cool.

3. When the toffee has cooled, temper the chocolate (see page 149). Spread a thick layer of the chocolate on top of the toffee. Sprinkle the nuts on top and let set until the chocolate is firm.

4. Break the toffee up into large or small pieces. Transfer the toffee pieces to cellophane bags, zipper-top plastic bags, or airtight containers. For special occasions, place the toffee in food-safe metal tins with layers separated by parchment or waxed paper.

1¼ cups packed light brown sugar

8 tablespoons (1 stick) unsalted butter, cut into small pieces

2 tablespoons water

1 tablespoon light corn syrup

1 teaspoon pure vanilla extract

¼ teaspoon baking soda

1 pound dark chocolate (60% to 70% cacao), roughly chopped

½ cup crushed toasted almonds or pistachios (see page 95)

Peppermint Fantasy Fudge

This easy fudge is adapted from a back-of-the-box recipe that some proclaim as the smoothest fudge. It's also much easier to make than the traditional kind and takes only about 10 minutes of active cooking time—a plus if you are especially swamped during the holidays. And it keeps for a month! MAKES 64 PIECES

1½ cups sugar

⅔ cup evaporated milk

2 tablespoons salted butter

¼ teaspoon kosher salt

2 cups miniature marshmallows

1½ cups semisweet or dark chocolate chips

1 teaspoon peppermint extract

¼ cup crushed candy canes or peppermint candies

1. Line an 8-inch square pan with aluminum foil or parchment paper, leaving extra for overhang; set aside.

2. In a heavy-bottomed 2-quart saucepan fitted with a candy thermometer, combine the sugar, milk, butter, and salt over medium heat. Stir with a wooden spoon or silicone spatula. As soon as the mixture reaches 234°F, remove the pan from the heat and quickly stir in the marshmallows, chocolate chips, and peppermint extract. Continue to stir until the marshmallows and chocolate chips have melted. Transfer the mixture to the prepared pan. Sprinkle the crushed candy over the fudge. Allow to cool at room temperature until set, about 2 hours.

3. Remove the fudge from the pan by grasping the extra foil or parchment paper and pulling the block of candy out. Peel the foil or paper away from the fudge and cut into 1-inch squares. Layer a shallow food-safe metal container with mini muffin papers or paper candy cups. Place the fudge in the cups. Fill the empty spaces of the container with pieces of crumpled parchment or waxed paper before covering.

Candy Thermometers

Though candy thermometers are not a necessity for making candy, they make things a lot easier. I like using a metal thermometer with a clip that attaches to the side of the pot. It's inexpensive, can be purchased in most kitchen-supply or department stores, and can also be used for deep-frying.

Happy Hours

Inspired by bar snacks and drinks, these sweet and salty bites are the perfect treat to send to anyone who likes to kick back with a cold one after work. Try a variety of beers to see which ones you like best, since they can impart varying levels of bitterness or richness to the caramel. These caramels keep for 1 month.

MAKES 64 CARAMELS

2 cups mini pretzels (about 40 pretzels)

¾ cup Beer Nuts or lightly salted peanuts

1 (12-ounce) bottle brown ale, India pale ale, or stout

1 cup heavy cream

1¼ cups sugar

¼ cup light corn syrup

2 tablespoons unsalted butter

1. Line an 8-inch square pan with parchment paper, leaving extra for overhang. Scatter the pretzels and nuts over the bottom of the pan; set aside.

2. Pour the beer into a heavy-bottomed 2-quart saucepan and let it sit until flat, about 30 minutes.

3. Bring the beer to a boil over medium-high heat and continue to cook, stirring occasionally, until reduced to about 2 tablespoons, 20 to 25 minutes.

4. In a large, heavy-bottomed saucepan fitted with a candy thermometer, combine the beer reduction, cream, sugar, corn syrup, and butter. Bring the mixture to a boil over medium-high heat and cook, stirring occasionally, until the mixture reaches 245°F, 10 to 12 minutes. Quickly pour the caramel into the prepared pan and allow the mixture to cool completely, about 2 hours.

4. Grasping the parchment paper, remove the caramel from the pan and place on a cutting board. Using a sharp knife, cut the caramels into 1-inch squares. Wrap in candy wrappers, waxed paper, or parchment paper and pack the caramels in zipper-top plastic bags or airtight containers.

Honey Granola Bars

Instead of using a square pan for these bars, I've opted for two 5 x 9-inch loaf pans because the shape is perfect for granola bars and eliminates the possibility of odd shapes. When you cut the bars across the width of the pan, you end up with bars that are about 5 inches long and about 1 inch wide—similar in size to the packaged granola bars you can buy at the supermarket. These bars will keep for up to 10 days. **MAKES 12 BARS**

1. Preheat the oven to 350°F. Line two 5 x 9-inch loaf pans with parchment paper, leaving extra for overhang; set aside.

2. In a medium-size bowl, combine the oats, sunflower seeds, wheat germ, and salt.

3. In a small, heavy-bottomed saucepan over medium heat, heat the honey, oil, and maple syrup. When the mixture comes to a simmer, remove the pan from heat and stir in the vanilla. Pour the mixture over the oats and stir until the oats are completely coated. Pour the oat mixture into the prepared pans and firmly press the mixture into the bottom of the pans. Bake until the edges begin to brown, 20 to 25 minutes.

4. Let cool in the pans on a rack. While the bars are still slightly warm, remove them from the pans by grasping the parchment paper. Cut each loaf crosswise into 6 bars, for a total of 12 bars, and transfer them to a rack to cool completely. Wrap the bars individually with waxed or parchment paper or plastic wrap, seal with tape, and pack in a zipper-top plastic bag. Alternatively, layer unwrapped bars in an airtight container, separating the layers with waxed or parchment paper.

2 cups old-fashioned rolled oats

1 cup salted or unsalted sunflower seeds

2 tablespoons toasted wheat germ

Pinch of salt

½ cup honey

6 tablespoons vegetable or canola oil

¼ cup pure maple syrup

½ teaspoon pure vanilla extract

Whole-Wheat Almond *and* Orange Biscotti

Twice baked, these dunkable Italian cookies are perfect for long layovers because of their sturdy texture. Firm and crisp, they hold their shape when jostled around in a box and literally won't go stale. (They're best within 3 weeks, though.) They make a great treat any time of day. **MAKES ABOUT 5 DOZEN BISCOTTI**

1½ cups all-purpose flour

1½ cups whole-wheat flour

4 teaspoons baking powder

7 tablespoons unsalted butter, at room temperature

1 cup sugar

3 large eggs, at room temperature

2 tablespoons freshly grated orange zest

2 tablespoons freshly squeezed orange juice

2 teaspoons pure almond extract

1 cup coarsely chopped unsalted almonds

Sparkling sugar (optional)

1. Preheat the oven to 350°F. Line two baking sheets with parchment paper or silicone baking liners; set aside.

2. In a medium-size bowl, combine the flours and baking powder.

3. In the bowl of an electric mixer, beat the butter and sugar on medium speed until light and fluffy. Add the eggs and mix until well blended. Add the orange zest, juice, and almond extract, and mix again until blended, periodically scraping down the sides of the bowl. Add the flour mixture and mix on low speed until combined. Fold in the almonds. The dough should be wet and sticky.

4. Transfer the dough to a lightly floured surface and divide in half. Using floured hands, shape each half into a 16-inch log. Brush off excess flour and transfer the logs to the prepared baking sheets. Flatten each log so that it is 2 inches wide. Sprinkle with sparkling sugar, if desired.

5. Bake until golden and firm to the touch, about 30 minutes. Let cool completely on the baking sheets. Reduce the oven temperature to 300°F.

6. Transfer the cooled logs to a work surface. Using a serrated knife, cut on the diagonal into ½-inch-thick slices. Arrange the biscotti, cut side down, on the baking sheets. Bake until the cookies are dry and golden brown, about 25 minutes, turning the biscotti over halfway through.

7. Transfer the biscotti to a rack and let them cool completely. Pack in zipper-top plastic bags, pressing out any air, or in airtight containers, separating the layers with waxed or parchment paper.

Brown Sugar Crisps

These crisp cookies are a hybrid of a brown sugar–based icebox cookie and speculoos, a Belgian spiced cookie. "Speculoos" can refer to either the cookie or to a spread that's similar in appearance to peanut butter. The cinnamon-based cookies have been a staple in Belgium for more than 100 years and have become increasingly available in the United States. When stored properly, these sturdy cookies keep for 3 weeks. **MAKES 8 TO 9 DOZEN COOKIES**

1. In a medium-size bowl, combine the flour, almonds, baking soda, salt, and spices.

2. In the bowl of an electric mixer, beat the butter and sugar on medium speed until light and fluffy. Add the egg and vanilla and mix again until combined. Add the flour mixture and mix until incorporated. Divide the dough in half and transfer the dough pieces to waxed or parchment paper. Shape each half into a round log 12 to 14 inches long and 1½ inches in diameter. Wrap the log and twist the ends of the paper so that each log becomes a cylinder, and refrigerate for at least 1 hour.

3. Preheat the oven to 350°F. Line two baking sheets with parchment paper or silicone baking liners; set aside.

4. Remove the cookie dough from the paper and slice into ¼-inch-thick pieces. Place the pieces on the baking sheets, about 2 inches apart. Bake until the edges are firm and golden brown, 10 to 12 minutes.

5. Let the cookies cool on the pans for 5 minutes before transferring them to a rack to cool completely. Pack in zipper-top plastic bags, pressing out any air, or in airtight containers, separating the layers with waxed or parchment paper.

1½ cups all-purpose flour

½ cup chopped slivered almonds

½ teaspoon baking soda

¼ teaspoon salt

¼ teaspoon ground cinnamon

⅛ teaspoon ground ginger

⅛ teaspoon ground nutmeg

8 tablespoons (1 stick) unsalted butter, at room temperature

1 cup packed light brown sugar

1 large egg, at room temperature

¾ teaspoon pure vanilla extract

Green Tea Shortbread Bites

Matcha is a powder made from finely ground green tea leaves. It can be purchased at Asian specialty shops, health food stores, or online. In recent years, researchers have discovered that green tea extract acts as a natural preservative in foods. While the tea powder has a functional property, helping these cookies stay fresh for up to 3 weeks, it also lends a delicate vegetal flavor. **MAKES ABOUT 8 DOZEN COOKIES**

2½ cups all-purpose flour

1 tablespoon matcha green tea powder

1 tablespoon baking powder

½ teaspoon salt

10 tablespoons (1¼ sticks) unsalted butter, at room temperature

1 cup sugar

1 large egg, at room temperature

¼ cup milk

12 ounces white chocolate (chips or chopped-up bars)

1. In a medium-size bowl, sift together the flour, matcha powder, baking powder, and salt.

2. In the bowl of an electric mixer, beat the butter and sugar on medium speed until light and fluffy. Add the egg and beat until combined. Alternate adding the flour mixture and the milk, mixing well after each addition, until all is incorporated.

3. Divide the dough into two equal pieces and transfer them to two pieces of waxed or parchment paper. Shape the dough into rectangular logs 12 to 14 inches in length and 1½ inches square. Wrap the dough logs and refrigerate for at least 2 hours.

4. Preheat the oven to 375°F. Line two baking sheets with parchment paper or silicone baking liners; set aside.

5. Remove the dough from the refrigerator and slice into ¼-inch-thick pieces. Place on prepared baking sheets, about 1 inch apart. Bake until the edges are slightly brown, 6 to 8 minutes. Let cool on the baking sheets. Repeat with the remaining dough.

6. Place the white chocolate in a medium-size heatproof bowl. Place the bowl over a pot of simmering water and continually stir the chocolate, making sure that water does not come into contact with the chocolate. When the chocolate is melted, dip one-third of each cooled cookie into the melted white chocolate. Let the dipped shortbread set completely on a rack before packing the cookies in airtight containers, separating the layers with waxed or parchment paper.

Salted Nut Brittle

Brittle is a terrific candy to include in care packages. Not only does it keep for long periods of time (this one for up to 1 month), but it's also supposed to be broken into irregular pieces, easing any concerns of breakage resulting from rough handling. Layer the brittle in airtight tins or make small bundles of the candy with cellophane bags. **MAKES ABOUT 1 POUND BRITTLE**

1. Line a baking sheet with parchment paper or a silicone baking liner; set aside.

2. In a medium-size heavy-bottomed saucepan fitted with a candy thermometer, combine the sugar, water, butter, and corn syrup. Heat over medium heat until the sugar is dissolved, stirring occasionally with a wooden spoon. Cook until the mixture bubbles and registers 295°F.

3. Remove the pan from the heat and quickly stir in the nuts. Add the baking soda and salt, and stir until combined. The mixture will bubble and expand in volume.

4. Pour the mixture onto the prepared baking sheet and spread out with a spoon or heatproof spatula to about ¼ inch thick. Allow the brittle to cool until it has hardened, about 30 minutes. Break into pieces. Transfer to airtight containers, zipper-top plastic bags, or cellophane bags.

1 cup packed light brown sugar

¼ cup water

4 tablespoons (½ stick) salted butter

2 tablespoons light corn syrup

1 cup toasted nuts, such as pistachios, salted peanuts, and/or slivered almonds (see box below)

1 teaspoon baking soda

¼ teaspoon kosher salt

Toasting Nuts

Toasted nuts can add an intense flavor, crunchy texture, and nice golden color to dishes. To toast, spread nuts in a single layer on a baking sheet and toast in a 350°F oven for 5 to 15 minutes, shaking the pan occasionally, until they are golden and fragrant. Toasting time can vary widely depending on the type of nut, so watch the nuts carefully to make sure they do not burn. You can also toast nuts in a dry skillet on the stovetop. This technique is convenient for small quantities of nuts, but if you're not watching closely and the heat is too high, the nuts can burn very quickly.

Cherry, Hazelnut, *and* Pistachio Nougat

Adapted from one of my go-to cookbooks, *The Joy of Cooking*, this nougat incorporates some of my favorite fruits and nuts to create a gooey candy that keeps for up to 1 month. You can wrap these firm and chewy treats in waxed or parchment paper or in candy wrappers, which are available in craft or specialty stores. The colorful nougat is great for sending to loved ones around the holidays. **MAKES 64 PIECES**

1½ cups sugar

1¼ cups light corn syrup

½ cup water

2 large egg whites, at room temperature

2 tablespoons unsalted butter, at room temperature

½ teaspoon pure almond extract

½ cup toasted pistachios (see page 95)

½ cup toasted skinned hazelnuts (see page 95)

⅔ cup dried tart cherries

1. Line an 8-inch square pan with parchment paper or foil, leaving extra for overhang. Grease the paper or foil; set aside.

2. In a heavy-bottomed 2-quart saucepan fitted with a candy thermometer, combine the sugar, corn syrup, and water. Heat over low heat, stirring, until the sugar is dissolved. Increase the heat to medium and bring the mixture to a boil. Cook, without stirring, until it reaches 275°F. At first, the mixture will bubble and almost appear to bubble over, but it will quickly subside.

3. Meanwhile, in the bowl of an electric mixer, whip the egg whites until stiff peaks form. As soon as the syrup reaches 275°F, remove the pan from the heat. With the mixer on high, carefully pour the hot syrup into the egg whites. Avoid pouring the mixture onto the beaters, as it may splatter. Continue to beat on high for 10 minutes. The mixture will look smooth and glossy.

4. Beat in the butter and almond extract. The mixture will look a bit curdled at first, but it will even out after beating for about 30 seconds. Fold in the nuts and fruit. Spread the mixture in the prepared pan and set it aside at room temperature to cool completely.

5. Cut the nougat into 1-inch squares. Wrap the nougat pieces in candy wrappers, waxed paper, or parchment paper and pack in zipper-top plastic bags or airtight containers.

Candy Wrappers

Although it's easy enough to make your own candy wrappers by cutting up pieces of parchment or waxed paper, you can also purchase candy wrappers in various shapes, sizes, and colors at craft stores or through the Internet. These ready-made wrappers come in handy when you have a lot of candies to wrap.

Spiced Cocoa-Dusted Nuts

Coated with a crispy, sweet crust and then dusted with dark cocoa powder, these sweet and spicy nuts will keep for a month when stored in a cool, dark place. They make great Halloween gifts for your favorite faraway trick-or-treater or for your long-distance (or nearby!) sweetie at Valentine's Day. Pack them in cellophane bags and seal with seasonal stickers or ribbons. **MAKES ABOUT 3 CUPS NUTS**

⅔ cup sugar

¼ cup water

1 teaspoon ground cinnamon

½ teaspoon cayenne pepper

2½ cups unsalted mixed roasted nuts of your choice, such as hazelnuts, peanuts, almonds, and/or pecans

12 ounces semisweet chocolate, chopped

½ cup Dutch-processed cocoa powder, sifted

1. In a medium-size saucepan over medium heat, stir together the sugar, water, cinnamon, and cayenne. Add the nuts and continue to stir until the sugar begins to crystallize and harden. Remove the pan from the heat, spread the mixture evenly on two baking sheets, and let cool.

2. Meanwhile, place the chocolate in a heatproof bowl and place the bowl over a pot of simmering water. Stir the chocolate until it is melted. Remove from the heat. Add the cooled nuts to the chocolate and stir to coat.

3. Line the two baking sheets with parchment paper or silicone baking liners. Using a fork or slotted spoon, pull the nuts out of the chocolate and set on the sheet pans, separating them as necessary. Transfer the sheet pans to the freezer and let the chocolate set, about 15 minutes.

4. Put the cocoa powder in a medium-size bowl. In small batches, toss the chocolate-covered nuts in the cocoa. Put the nuts in a colander and then shake the excess cocoa off. Pack the nuts in small cellophane bags, zipper-top plastic bags, or candy tins. If packing in tins, first place the nuts in zipper-top plastic bags to keep out moisture.

Chocolate-Ginger Rum Balls

Not only does the addition of rum make these treats more festive and fit for the holiday season, it also helps keep them fresh for 2 to 3 weeks. Alcohol is a preservative that is known to help keep foods longer and make them taste better as they age (think fruitcake). **MAKES ABOUT 4 DOZEN BALLS**

1. Place the semisweet chocolate in a heatproof bowl set over a pot of simmering water. Stir the chocolate until it is melted. Remove the bowl from the heat and stir in the sugar, rum, corn syrup, and ginger. Mix until well combined.

2. In the bowl of a food processor, process the gingersnaps and walnuts until finely ground. Add the chocolate mixture to the bowl and process again until well blended. Transfer the mixture to a bowl and chill in the refrigerator for at least 1 hour.

3. Line a baking sheet with waxed or parchment paper. Using your hands, roll the mixture into 1-inch balls and place them on the prepared baking sheet.

4. Place the cocoa powder on a plate and roll the balls in it. Alternatively, temper the bittersweet chocolate according to the instructions on page 149 and dip the balls in the tempered chocolate. Let the balls set at room temperature on a rack. Layer a shallow food-safe metal container with mini muffin liner cups or candy cups. Place the balls in the cups. Fill the empty spaces of the container with pieces of crumpled parchment or waxed paper before covering.

1 cup semisweet chocolate chips

½ cup sugar

⅓ cup dark or light rum

3 tablespoons light corn syrup

¼ cup finely chopped crystallized ginger

40 gingersnap cookies

1¼ cups walnut halves

¾ cup natural unsweetened cocoa powder or 12 ounces bittersweet chocolate

Post-Holiday Sales

Post-holiday sales in January are the best opportunities to get great deals on decorative tins and cookie decorating items like ribbons, tags, festive muffin cup liners, and candy bags. They are usually marked down 50 percent or more. It's worth stocking up!

Cinnamon-Spice Popcorn

Inspired by the sweet and savory taste of kettle corn, I created a slight variation on the treat by adding ground cinnamon. Made in minutes on the stovetop, this quick and easy snack is a great gift. And, when stored properly, it will keep for up to 3 weeks. Package the popcorn in individual serving bags or in a large tin for sharing. **MAKES ABOUT 8 CUPS POPCORN**

2 tablespoons vegetable or canola oil

⅓ cup popcorn kernels

Scant ¼ cup sugar

1 tablespoon ground cinnamon

¼ teaspoon kosher salt

1. In a large saucepan over medium-high heat, heat the oil. Add the popcorn kernels and scatter the sugar over the kernels. Cover the pot with a tight-fitting lid. After the kernels begin to pop, shake the pan continuously until the popping subsides, 2 to 3 minutes. Remove from the heat.

2. Lift the lid and sprinkle the cinnamon and salt over the popcorn. Cover and shake vigorously to coat the popcorn with the seasonings.

3. Allow the popcorn to cool completely. Fill quart-size zipper-top plastic bags with individual portions or pack the popcorn in one large airtight container.

Caramel-Pecan Popcorn Balls

If you do not have a popcorn popper, you can easily make healthy homemade popcorn in the microwave. All you need is a paper bag and popcorn kernels. Simply take a clean paper bag and scatter a few tablespoons of popcorn kernels inside. Fold the open end of the bag shut, place the bag on its side in the microwave, and cook on high power for 3 to 4 minutes or until the pops begin to subside. Remove the popcorn from the bag and discard any unpopped kernels. These sweet popcorn balls will keep for at least 1 week. **MAKES ABOUT 10 POPCORN BALLS**

1. In a large bowl, combine the popcorn, pecans, and cranberries.

2. In a small saucepan over low heat, warm the cream, butter, and salt; do not boil. At the same time, in a heavy-bottomed 2-quart saucepan fitted with a candy thermometer, bring the sugar and corn syrup to a boil over medium-high heat. When the sugar becomes light amber in color, slowly add the warm cream mixture and bring the caramel up to 240°F. Remove the pan from the heat and stir in the vanilla and cinnamon. Pour the mixture over the popcorn and quickly stir to coat evenly.

3. When the popcorn mixture is cool enough to handle, form baseball-size popcorn balls with buttered hands. Wrap the balls individually in waxed paper or colored/decorative plastic wrap and tie with a ribbon. Pack the balls in an airtight container or zipper-top plastic bag.

10 cups air-popped popcorn (from about ⅓ cup unpopped kernels)

1 cup chopped toasted pecans (see page 95)

½ cup dried cranberries

½ cup heavy cream

1 tablespoon unsalted butter

Pinch of salt

½ cup sugar

¼ cup light corn syrup

½ teaspoon pure vanilla extract

¼ teaspoon ground cinnamon

Cinnamon Marshmallows

They may seem intimidating, but once you make fresh marshmallows, it's hard to go back to the bagged variety. Plus, they ship amazingly well because of their forgiving texture and will keep for more than a month! Pack them in cellophane gift bags and tie with decorative ribbons for a swanky-looking gift. You can also package them with the S'mores Kit on page 163. **MAKES ABOUT 10 DOZEN MARSHMALLOWS**

½ cup confectioners' sugar, sifted, plus more if needed

4 (1-ounce) packets unflavored powdered gelatin

¾ cup cold water

¼ cup hot water

2 cups sugar

¾ cup light corn syrup

¼ teaspoon kosher salt

1 tablespoon pure vanilla extract

1 tablespoon natural unsweetened cocoa powder (optional)

1 teaspoon ground cinnamon

1. Grease a 9 x 13-inch pan and then coat with confectioners' sugar.

2. In a small bowl, mix the gelatin with ¼ cup of the cold water. Let stand for 5 minutes. Add the ¼ cup hot water and stir to dissolve completely. Transfer the gelatin to the bowl of an electric mixer fitted with a whip attachment; set aside.

3. In a medium-size saucepan fitted with a candy thermometer, combine the sugar, corn syrup, the remaining ½ cup cold water, and the salt over low heat. When dissolved, increase the heat to medium-high. As soon as the temperature reaches 245°F, remove the pan from the heat.

4. With the mixer on medium speed, pour the hot sugar syrup into the gelatin in a slow and steady stream. Be very careful, since the syrup is extremely hot. Try to avoid pouring the liquid directly onto the whip, since it may splatter. Beat until fully mixed, 8 to 10 minutes. It will become more voluminous and have a shiny sheen.

5. Add the vanilla, cocoa (if using), and cinnamon, and mix for another minute. Using a nonstick spatula, scrape the marshmallow mixture out of the bowl and into the prepared pan. With buttered or greased hands, spread the mixture evenly in the pan. Let cool at room temperature until the mixture firms up, at least 4 hours.

6. Sprinkle confectioners' sugar on top of the marshmallows before slicing into 1-inch squares. Toss the marshmallows with more confectioners' sugar to prevent them from sticking to one another. Pack in airtight containers, separating the layers with waxed paper, or in decorative bags.

No-Bake Swedish Coco Balls

These simple treats are similar to a snack I once had at a coffee shop in Brooklyn. After some tinkering at home, I was able to create a similar sweet that keeps for more than a week without refrigeration. When packing these for shipment, line a tin with mini cupcake papers, place a coco ball in each cup, and cover with waxed paper to fill the tin and prevent shifting. Tie the tin with a nice ribbon and pack in a box with sufficient cushioning. **MAKES ABOUT 2 DOZEN BALLS**

1. Place the chopped chocolate in a microwave-safe bowl. Microwave on high power for 10 seconds. Remove from the microwave and stir. If the chocolate is not completely melted and smooth, continue to microwave in 10-second increments and then stir again.

2. In a large bowl, combine the oats, sugar, cocoa powder, and cardamom. Add the butter to the oat mixture and work it into the mixture with your fingertips until well combined. Stir in the brewed coffee, vanilla, and melted chocolate. Refrigerate for 30 minutes, or until chilled.

3. Using a cookie dough scoop or your hands, form dough balls about 1½ inches in diameter. If you are using nuts, mix the coconut and nuts together on a plate and roll the dough balls in the mixture; otherwise, just roll the balls in the coconut.

4. Pack in an airtight container, separating the layers with waxed or parchment paper. Alternatively, layer a shallow food-safe metal container with mini muffin liner cups or candy cups. Place the balls in the cups. Fill the empty spaces of the container with pieces of crumpled parchment or waxed paper before covering.

1 ounce bittersweet chocolate (60% to 70% cacao), chopped

2 cups old-fashioned rolled oats

½ cup sugar

¼ cup natural unsweetened cocoa powder

½ teaspoon ground cardamom

8 tablespoons (1 stick) salted butter, softened

2 tablespoons brewed coffee or espresso, or rum

½ teaspoon pure vanilla extract

½ cup unsweetened finely shredded coconut

½ cup chopped toasted almonds or hazelnuts (optional; see page 95)

PACKABLE LOAVES *and* BREADS

Years ago, my husband's parents sent him half a cake to celebrate his birthday. Why he wasn't deserving of an entire cake is still the subject of lighthearted jabs, but their reasoning was that the entire cake didn't fit in the box. (My husband thinks they wanted to keep some for themselves!) With the recipes in this chapter, size won't be much of an issue, since these quick breads and cakes are compact and in manageable loaf or muffin shapes, which also makes them easier to ship. Wrap loaves, muffins, and small treats tightly in plastic wrap and then place in zipper-top plastic bags before shipping. This double wrapping will keep the treats moist and fresh. Alternatively, bake the loaf in a disposable aluminum or oven-safe paper pan and then wrap the cooled cake (still in the pan) in plastic wrap.

Carrot-Zucchini Muffins

These little wonders stay moist for 5 days thanks to the combination of carrots, zucchini, and raisins. These ingredients also provide color and a bit of natural sweetness to the muffins. You can use a box grater or the shredding disk on a food processor to grate the vegetables. Wrap the muffins individually so more of their moisture is retained during shipping. **MAKES 2 DOZEN MUFFINS**

3 cups all-purpose flour

1 teaspoon baking soda

¼ teaspoon baking powder

1 teaspoon kosher salt

½ teaspoon ground cinnamon

½ teaspoon ground nutmeg

1 cup vegetable or canola oil

1¾ cups sugar

3 large eggs, at room temperature

2 teaspoons pure vanilla extract

1 cup coarsely grated carrots

1 cup coarsely grated zucchini

1 cup raisins

1. Preheat the oven to 325°F. Grease two 12-cup muffin pans or line with cupcake liners; set aside.

2. In a medium-size bowl, combine the flour, baking soda, baking powder, salt, cinnamon, and nutmeg.

3. In the bowl of an electric mixer, mix the oil and sugar on medium speed until blended. Add the eggs and vanilla, and mix until incorporated, scraping down the sides of the bowl if necessary. Add the flour mixture and mix on low speed until blended. Fold in the carrots, zucchini, and raisins.

4. Fill the cups of the muffin pan two-thirds full. Bake until a toothpick inserted into the center of the muffins comes out clean, 20 to 22 minutes.

5. Cool the muffins in the pan for 5 minutes before transferring to a rack to cool completely. Wrap each muffin with plastic wrap and then pack the muffins in an airtight container or zipper-top plastic bag.

Chocolate Chip and Coconut Banana Bread

Classic banana bread is a treat that undoubtedly conjures up warm and sunny mornings. I've put a tropical spin on this version by adding coconut, along with chocolate chips. The additions complement the banana flavor and add extra sweetness to the bread. This bread keeps for 5 days and it freezes very well, so you can make it ahead and keep it on hand for when you need to put together a care package very quickly. Just be sure to bring the loaf to room temperature before packing to avoid excess condensation, which can promote the growth of mold.

MAKES 1 LOAF, SERVING 10 TO 12

1. Preheat the oven to 350°F. Grease and flour the bottom of a 5 x 9-inch loaf pan or line with parchment paper; set aside.

2. In a medium-size bowl, whisk together the flour, baking soda, cinnamon, and salt.

3. In the bowl of an electric mixer, beat the sugar and eggs on medium speed until light and airy. Add the bananas, oil, and vanilla, and mix until well combined, scraping down the sides of the bowl if necessary. Fold in the flour mixture. When well combined, fold in the chocolate chips and coconut. Pour the mixture into the prepared pan and bake until a toothpick inserted into the center of the bread comes out clean, 55 minutes to 1 hour.

4. Allow the bread to cool in the pan for 10 minutes, then transfer to a rack to cool completely. Wrap tightly with plastic wrap and place in a zipper-top plastic bag.

1⅔ cups all-purpose flour

1 teaspoon baking soda

½ teaspoon ground cinnamon

½ teaspoon salt

¾ cup sugar

2 large eggs, at room temperature

1½ cups mashed ripe bananas (about 3 large bananas)

½ cup vegetable or canola oil

1½ teaspoons pure vanilla extract

½ cup semisweet chocolate chips

1 cup sweetened shredded coconut

Earl Grey–Meyer Lemon Tea Bread

Meyer lemons are a cross between lemons and mandarin oranges. Paired with Earl Grey tea, the cake yields a lovely floral flavor and aroma. If you can't get Meyer lemons, use regular lemons or a combination of lemons and oranges. Although tea breads are often delicate, the dense texture of this bread, which keeps for 5 days, allows it to withstand the rigors of shipping without falling apart. **MAKES 1 LOAF, SERVING 10 TO 12**

1½ cups all-purpose flour

1 teaspoon baking powder

¼ teaspoon salt

6 tablespoons (¾ stick) unsalted butter, at room temperature

1 cup sugar

2 large eggs, at room temperature

1½ tablespoons freshly grated Meyer lemon zest (from about 4 lemons)

1½ teaspoons Earl Grey tea leaves (from 1½ teabags)

¼ cup milk

¼ cup sour cream

1 tablespoon freshly squeezed Meyer lemon juice

1. Preheat the oven to 325°F. Grease and flour a 5 x 9-inch loaf pan or line with parchment paper; set aside.

2. In a medium-size bowl, combine the flour, baking powder, and salt.

3. In the bowl of an electric mixer, beat the butter and sugar on medium speed until light and fluffy. Add the eggs, lemon zest, and tea leaves, and mix until combined. Add the milk, sour cream, and lemon juice; mix again until combined, scraping down the sides of the bowl if necessary. Add the flour mixture and mix on low speed until just combined. Transfer the batter to the prepared pan, and bake until a toothpick inserted into the middle of the loaf comes out clean, 40 to 45 minutes.

4. Let the bread cool in the pan for 10 minutes before transferring to a rack to cool completely. Wrap tightly with plastic wrap and place in a zipper-top plastic bag.

Almond-Pear Bread

The secret to keeping this bread moist is the grated pears. I use firm, unpeeled Bartlett pears, but you can try using other types such as Anjou or Bosc. It's best to use slightly underripe pears since they won't turn to mush when you grate them. This bread keeps for 5 days. **MAKES 1 LOAF, SERVING 10 TO 12**

1. Preheat the oven to 350°F. Grease and flour a 5 x 9-inch loaf pan or line with parchment paper; set aside.

2. In a medium-size bowl, combine the flour, ground almonds, baking soda, and salt.

3. In the bowl of an electric mixer, beat the butter and sugar on medium speed until light and fluffy. Add the eggs and almond extract and beat again until combined. Alternate adding the milk and the flour mixture, mixing well on low speed after each addition, until all is incorporated. Fold in the pears. Pour the batter into the prepared pan and top with the sliced almonds. Bake until a toothpick inserted into the center of the bread comes out clean, 1 hour to 1 hour and 10 minutes.

4. Cool the bread in the pan for 10 minutes before transferring to a rack to cool completely. Wrap tightly with plastic wrap and place in a zipper-top plastic bag.

1½ cups all-purpose flour

1 cup finely chopped almonds (pulse ¾ cup whole almonds in a food processor)

1 teaspoon baking soda

½ teaspoon salt

⅓ cup unsalted butter, at room temperature

1 cup sugar

2 large eggs, at room temperature

1½ teaspoons pure almond extract

½ cup milk

1 cup grated pears, liquid squeezed out

2 tablespoons sliced almonds

Coffee *and* Spice Doughnut Loaf

The flavors of coffee and doughnuts come together in this sweet treat. I've infused this loaf bread with cinnamon and nutmeg, added an espresso-flavored swirl to provide some palate-pleasing bitterness, and then topped it with cinnamon sugar for a sweet crunch. Send this breakfast of champions to the early bird in your life. It will keep for 5 days. **MAKES 1 LOAF, SERVING 10 TO 12**

2½ cups all-purpose flour

1 teaspoon baking soda

½ teaspoon salt

½ teaspoon ground nutmeg

¾ teaspoon ground cinnamon

½ cup vegetable or canola oil

¾ cup packed light brown sugar

½ cup plus 2 tablespoons granulated sugar

1 cup buttermilk

2 large eggs, at room temperature

1 tablespoon instant espresso powder or coffee granules

1. Preheat the oven to 350°F. Grease and flour a 5 x 9-inch loaf pan or line with parchment paper; set aside.

2. In a medium-size bowl, combine the flour, baking soda, salt, nutmeg, and ½ teaspoon of the cinnamon.

3. In a large bowl, mix the oil, brown sugar, and ½ cup of the granulated sugar until combined, then add the buttermilk and eggs. Stir until the ingredients are well blended. Add the flour mixture and mix until incorporated.

4. Transfer 1 cup of the batter to a small bowl. Add the espresso powder and stir until combined. It's okay if the granules aren't completely dissolved. Pour the remaining batter into the prepared loaf pan and spoon dollops of the espresso-flavored batter onto the batter. Using a skewer or chopstick, swirl the batters together gently to create a marbleized effect.

5. In a small bowl, combine the remaining 2 tablespoons granulated sugar with the remaining ¼ teaspoon cinnamon. Sprinkle over the top of the batter. Bake until a toothpick inserted into the center of the loaf comes out clean, 55 minutes to 1 hour.

6. Cool the bread in the pan for 10 minutes before transferring to a rack to cool completely. Wrap tightly with plastic wrap and place in a zipper-top plastic bag.

Yogurt *and* Sour Cream Lemon Cake

The flavors of yogurt and sour cream are so subtle in this cake that you'll barely taste them. However, they keep the cake moist and tender for 5 days. Make sure to wrap the cake securely in plastic wrap before shipping—this will keep it from falling apart and losing moisture. **MAKES 1 LOAF, SERVING 10 TO 12**

2 cups all-purpose flour

1½ teaspoons baking powder

½ teaspoon baking soda

¼ teaspoon salt

⅓ cup vegetable or canola oil

1 cup sugar

½ cup plain whole-fat yogurt

½ cup whole-fat sour cream

2 large eggs, at room temperature

1 tablespoon freshly grated lemon zest

½ teaspoon pure vanilla extract

1. Preheat the oven to 350°F. Grease and flour a 5 x 9-inch loaf pan or line with parchment paper; set aside.

2. In a medium-size bowl, combine the flour, baking powder, baking soda, and salt.

3. In the bowl of an electric mixer, beat the oil and sugar on medium speed until combined. Add the yogurt and sour cream. Mix again until well blended. Add the eggs, lemon zest, and vanilla; mix again, scraping down the sides of the bowl if necessary. Add the flour mixture and mix on low speed until combined. Pour the batter into the prepared pan and bake until a toothpick inserted into the center of the cakes comes out clean, 55 minutes to 1 hour.

4. Cool the cake in the pan for 10 minutes before transferring to a rack to cool completely. Wrap tightly with plastic wrap and place in a zipper-top plastic bag.

Lighten Up

For most recipes, you can substitute low-fat or nonfat varieties of yogurt and sour cream, but the flavor will not be as rich.

Cardamom-Orange Coffee Cake Loaf

This loaf is a modified version of traditional coffee cake. Instead of baking the cake in a ring pan, I used a loaf pan because the finished shape is sturdier for shipping. I also used a lighter topping for the crust, which reduces the chance of crumbling during transport. This cake will keep for 5 days. **MAKES 1 LOAF, SERVING 10 TO 12**

1. Preheat the oven to 350°F. Grease and flour a 5 x 9-inch loaf pan or line with parchment paper; set aside.

2. Make the cake: In a medium-size bowl, combine the flour, baking soda, cardamom, cinnamon, and salt.

3. In the bowl of an electric mixer, beat the butter and sugar on medium speed until light and fluffy. Add the eggs one at a time, mixing after each addition and scraping down the sides of the bowl if necessary. Add the sour cream and orange zest and mix for another minute or two, until incorporated. Add the flour mixture and mix on low speed until combined. Pour the batter into the prepared pan.

4. In a small bowl, combine the topping ingredients. Scatter the topping over the batter. Bake until a toothpick inserted into the center of the cake comes out clean, about 50 minutes.

5. Cool the cake in the pan for 10 minutes before transferring to a rack to cool completely. Wrap tightly in plastic wrap and place in a large zipper-top plastic bag.

CAKE

- 1¾ cups all purpose flour
- 1 teaspoon baking soda
- 2 teaspoons ground cardamom
- ½ teaspoon ground cinnamon
- ¼ teaspoon salt
- 8 tablespoons (1 stick) unsalted butter, at room temperature
- 1 cup sugar
- 2 large eggs, at room temperature
- ½ cup sour cream
- 1 tablespoon freshly grated orange zest

TOPPING

- 2 tablespoons sliced almonds
- 1 tablespoon sugar
- ¼ teaspoon ground cinnamon
- ¼ teaspoon ground cardamom

Orange-Bourbon Tipsy Cake

Rich and boozy, this cake is redolent of the "tipsy cake" I had when I first visited Tennessee. That cake was studded with plump raisins and pecans, and soaked with Jack Daniel's Tennessee Whiskey! While this cake comes close to containing the same amount of booze, I've developed a slightly modified version by using bourbon and orange peel. The alcohol in this adult treat helps keep the cake moist and provides a deep flavor that awakens taste buds. This keeps for 5 days. **MAKES 1 LOAF, SERVING 8 TO 10**

1. Preheat the oven to 325°F. Grease and flour a 4 x 8-inch loaf pan; set aside.

2. Make the cake: In a medium-size bowl, combine the flour, baking powder, and salt.

3. In another medium-size bowl, stir together the butter and brown sugar until combined. Add the eggs one at a time, stirring until each one is incorporated, and then add the vanilla. Add the bourbon and orange zest, and stir again. Add the flour mixture and stir until just combined. Fold in the raisins. Pour the batter into the prepared pan and bake until a toothpick inserted into the center of the cake comes out clean, 45 to 50 minutes. Allow the cake to cool in the pan on a rack.

4. While the cake is cooling, combine the glaze ingredients in a small bowl. Stir until well combined. Remove the cake from the pan and place on a rack. Using a chopstick or skewer, poke several holes into the cooled cake. Pour the glaze over the cake and let it set, about 20 minutes.

5. Wrap the cake tightly with plastic wrap and place in a zipper-top plastic bag.

CAKE

- 1 cup plus 2 tablespoons all-purpose flour
- 1 teaspoon baking powder
- ¼ teaspoon salt
- 8 tablespoons (1 stick) unsalted butter, melted
- 1 cup packed light brown sugar
- 2 large eggs, at room temperature
- 1 teaspoon pure vanilla extract
- ¼ cup bourbon
- 1 tablespoon freshly grated orange zest
- ½ cup raisins

GLAZE

- 1 tablespoon unsalted butter, melted
- ½ cup confectioners' sugar
- ½ tablespoon bourbon
- ¼ teaspoon pure vanilla extract

Autumn-Spiced Pumpkin Loaf

This fall favorite stays moist and delicious for 5 days because of the pumpkin. When buying canned pumpkin, make sure that you do not buy pumpkin pie mix, which is presweetened and flavored with spices. Feel free to make this loaf in the suggested pan or in three 2½ x 4-inch mini loaf pans. If you decide to use the mini pans, bake for 30 minutes and then check for doneness. If not done, continue to bake, checking for doneness every 5 minutes. **MAKES 1 LOAF, SERVING 10 TO 12**

1⅔ cups all-purpose flour

½ teaspoon baking soda

½ teaspoon baking powder

½ teaspoon salt

¾ teaspoon ground cinnamon

¾ teaspoon ground ginger

¾ teaspoon ground nutmeg

1 cup packed light or dark brown sugar

½ cup vegetable or canola oil

2 large eggs, at room temperature

1½ cups canned solid-pack pumpkin puree

1. Preheat the oven to 350°F. Grease and flour a 5 x 9-inch loaf pan or line with parchment paper; set aside.

2. In a medium-size bowl, combine the flour, baking soda, baking powder, salt, and spices.

3. In another medium-size bowl, combine the sugar, oil, eggs, and pumpkin. Stir until well combined. Add the flour mixture to the pumpkin mixture and continue to stir until just blended. Pour the batter into the prepared pan. Bake until a toothpick inserted into the center of the pan comes out clean, 50 to 55 minutes.

4. Cool the loaf in the pan for 10 minutes before transferring to a rack to cool completely. Wrap tightly with plastic wrap and place in a zipper-top plastic bag.

Apple, Molasses, *and* Ginger Bread

Fitting for the holidays, this delicious spice bread is flavored with a blend of four spices, molasses, and applesauce. Packed properly, this treat will survive bumpy rides and keep for 5 days. **MAKES 1 LOAF, SERVING 10 TO 12**

1. Preheat the oven to 350°F. Grease and flour a 5 x 9-inch loaf pan or line with parchment paper; set aside.

2. In a medium-size bowl, combine the flour, baking soda, salt, cinnamon, ground ginger, nutmeg, and cloves.

3. In the bowl of an electric mixer, mix the oil and brown sugar on medium speed. Add the egg, applesauce, buttermilk, molasses, and grated ginger; mix until well combined. Add the flour mixture and mix on low speed until combined. Pour the batter into the prepared pan and scatter the sparkling sugar on top. Bake until a toothpick inserted into the center of the bread comes out clean, 55 to 60 minutes.

4. Let the bread cool in the pan for 10 minutes before transferring to a rack to cool completely. Wrap tightly with plastic wrap and place in a zipper-top plastic bag.

2½ cups all-purpose flour

1½ teaspoons baking soda

1 teaspoon salt

2 teaspoons ground cinnamon

1½ teaspoons ground ginger

¼ teaspoon ground nutmeg

¼ teaspoon ground cloves

⅓ cup vegetable or canola oil

⅔ cup packed light brown sugar

1 large egg

1 cup sweetened applesauce

½ cup buttermilk

⅓ cup molasses

1 tablespoon freshly grated ginger

2 teaspoons sparkling sugar

Homemade Applesauce

If you have leftover apples, you can certainly make your own applesauce for this spice bread. Simply peel and core the apples and then chop into medium-size pieces. Place in a medium-size saucepan and cook on medium-low heat until the apples break down and soften, then add sugar to taste.

Double Chocolate Bread

Flavored with Dutch-processed cocoa and semisweet chocolate chips, this doubly delicious chocolate cake is rich, moist, and firm—perfect for shipping. It will keep for 5 days. Suggest that your recipient serve it with a strong cup of coffee or tea or just a tall glass of cold milk. **MAKES 1 LOAF, SERVING 10 TO 12**

1⅔ cups all-purpose flour

½ cup Dutch-processed cocoa powder, sifted

½ teaspoon baking soda

12 tablespoons (1½ sticks) unsalted butter, at room temperature

1 cup sugar

⅓ cup sour cream

2 large eggs, at room temperature

½ cup strong brewed coffee

1½ teaspoons pure vanilla extract

1 cup semisweet chocolate chips

1. Preheat the oven to 350°F. Grease and flour a 5 x 9-inch loaf pan or line with parchment paper; set aside.

2. In a medium-size bowl, combine the flour, cocoa, and baking soda.

3. In the bowl of an electric mixer, beat the butter and sugar on medium speed until light and fluffy. Add the sour cream and then the eggs, one at a time, mixing after each addition. Add the brewed coffee and vanilla. Mix for another minute or until the mixture is fully incorporated. Add the flour mixture and mix on low speed until combined. Fold in the chocolate chips. Pour the batter into the prepared pan. Bake until a toothpick inserted into the center of the bread comes out clean, 1 hour to 1 hour and 10 minutes.

4. Cool the bread in the pan for 10 minutes before transferring to a rack to cool completely. Wrap tightly with plastic wrap and place in a zipper-top plastic bag.

What Is Dutch-Processed Cocoa?

Dutch-processed, or alkalized, cocoa powder is cocoa that has had some of the natural acids removed during processing. The cocoa powder produced by this process is darker and richer in color and smoother and milder in flavor than natural cocoa.

Orange-Infused Irish Soda Bread

This bread is great as is, toasted, or slathered with high-quality butter. Because the loaf is low in fat, it can easily dry out if not stored properly. Take care to wrap the bread tightly with plastic wrap and place in a zipper-top plastic bag before shipping. It will keep for 1 week. **MAKES 1 LOAF, SERVING 8 TO 10**

1. Preheat the oven to 375°F. Grease a baking sheet or line with parchment paper or a silicone baking liner; set aside.

2. Put the raisins and orange juice in a small bowl and let sit for 10 minutes.

3. In a medium-size bowl, combine the flour, granulated sugar, baking powder, baking soda, and salt. Add the butter. With your fingertips, work the butter into the mixture until the pieces are as small as peas. Pour in the buttermilk and stir until well incorporated. Drain the raisins; squeeze out and discard the excess liquid. Add the raisins and orange zest to the dough and mix until blended. The dough will be sticky. Scrape the dough onto the prepared baking sheet and, with floured hands, shape the dough into a round loaf 8 to 9 inches in diameter. Sprinkle with the sparkling sugar.

4. Bake until a toothpick inserted into the center of the bread comes out clean, 30 to 35 minutes.

5. Cool the bread on the baking sheet for 10 minutes before transferring to a rack to cool completely. Wrap tightly with plastic wrap and place in a zipper-top plastic bag.

¾ cup raisins

1 cup orange juice, warmed

2 cups all-purpose flour

¼ cup granulated sugar

1½ teaspoons baking powder

1 teaspoon baking soda

1 teaspoon salt

3 tablespoons cold unsalted butter, cut into small pieces

1 cup buttermilk

1 tablespoon freshly grated orange zest

1 tablespoon sparkling sugar

Red Velvet Whoopie Pies

Traditional whoopie pies are filled with a white frosting that's usually made from shortening or butter. To make the pies more shelf stable, I've used marshmallows, which impart a sweet and luscious element to the treat. They keep for just 5 days, though, making them a good quick-ship choice. Marshmallow creme can also be used, but it is more viscous and can slowly spread out of the pies. Wrap these treats individually or in twos before shipping. **MAKES ABOUT 2 DOZEN MINIATURE PIES**

2 cups all-purpose flour

¼ cup natural unsweetened cocoa powder, sifted

1 teaspoon baking soda

½ teaspoon salt

8 tablespoons (1 stick) unsalted butter, at room temperature

1 cup packed light brown sugar

1 large egg, at room temperature

1 teaspoon pure vanilla extract

1 tablespoon red food coloring

¾ cup buttermilk

1 (10-ounce) bag full-size marshmallows

1. Preheat the oven to 350°F. Line two baking sheets with parchment paper or silicone baking liners; set aside.

2. In a medium-size bowl, combine the flour, cocoa powder, baking soda, and salt.

3. In the bowl of an electric mixer, beat the butter and sugar on medium speed until light and fluffy. Add the egg, vanilla, and food coloring, and mix until incorporated, scraping down the sides of the bowl if necessary. Alternate adding the buttermilk and flour mixture, mixing after each addition, until all is incorporated.

4. Drop 1-tablespoon scoops of the batter onto the prepared baking sheets, about 2 inches apart. Bake until the cakes spring back from being lightly pressed, 8 to 9 minutes. Allow the cakes to cool on the pans for 5 minutes before transferring to a rack to cool completely. Repeat with the remaining batter. Leave the oven on.

5. Arrange half of the cakes, flat side up, on the baking sheets and place a marshmallow on each cake. Return the pans to the oven and warm the marshmallows for about 5 minutes. They should puff up. Remove the pans from the oven and top each marshmallow with another cake, flat side down, to form a sandwich. Cool the whoopie pies on a rack.

6. Wrap each pie with plastic wrap and then place in a structured container, such as a small takeout container or metal tin, so they won't get crushed.

Triple Chocolate Cake Pops

People of all ages seem to love cake pops, but they make an especially great care package for a child—maybe a far-away niece or nephew who's celebrating a birthday. You can buy lollipop sticks or lollipop wrapping kits at most craft stores. Alternatively, you may skip the sticks and place the chocolate-dipped cake balls in mini cupcake papers or candy cups and then pack them in a tin. Tempering the chocolate will help it hold up better during shipping, and the chocolate coating will keep the cake centers moist and fresh for 5 days. **MAKES ABOUT 7 DOZEN CAKE POPS**

1. Line two baking sheets with waxed or parchment paper; set aside.

2. Break the cooled cake into coarse crumbs. Add the frosting and mix until blended. Refrigerate the mixture for 30 minutes. Using your hands, press and form the mixture into small balls, about 1 inch in diameter. Place the balls on the baking sheets and refrigerate for 1 hour to firm up.

3. While the cake balls are cooling, temper the chocolate (see page 149).

4. Poke a lollipop stick into the center of each cake ball. Holding the stick, dunk each ball into the tempered chocolate and then roll in any of the toppings, as desired. Insert the stick into the Styrofoam block. Let the chocolate set completely, about 10 minutes or longer if the chocolate layer is thick. (If you do not have lollipop sticks, you can stick the balls on the tines of a fork and then dunk them in the chocolate. Let set on a tray lined with parchment or waxed paper.)

5. Pack the cake pops in cellophane bags and secure with a twist tie or ribbon, then pack in an airtight container in layers separated by waxed paper.

1 (10.25-ounce) box of your favorite chocolate cake mix, prepared according to package directions, or 1 recipe Double Chocolate Bread (page 116), cooled completely

1 (16-ounce) container chocolate frosting

2 pounds dark chocolate (60% to 70% cacao), chopped

OPTIONAL TOPPINGS

Chocolate or colored sprinkles

Unsweetened shredded coconut, toasted (see box below)

White nonpareils

Mini chocolate chips

Special equipment: lollipop sticks, Styrofoam block or floral foam

Toasting Coconut

To toast shredded coconut, spread it in a shallow pan and toast at 375°F for 5 to 7 minutes, stirring occasionally.

SHIPPABLE SAVORIES

As someone with a serious sweet tooth, I've always found it strange that my parents prefer salty flavors over sweet. In fact, they've been known to sprinkle salt over fruit like watermelon, pineapple, and strawberries. For those who prefer savory over sweet, I've gathered some of my favorite savory snacks, such as Dickie's Nuts and Bolts and Sriracha Party Nuts. The treats in this chapter serve as a nice counterpoint to sugary treats in care packages. Since most of the snacks have a crunchy texture, it's wise to pack them carefully in airtight bags or containers so humidity won't soften them during shipping.

Whole-Grain Pita Chips

It's amazing how easy it is to make this healthy snack at home. It takes no more time than it would to go to the store to buy a bag. This is a very basic recipe, but try making jazzed-up variations with garlic or onion powder, dried herbs, spices like cumin or curry powder, or even cinnamon and sugar. If stored properly, these chips will keep for more than 2 weeks, so go ahead and ship them to your loved ones around the world. **MAKES ABOUT 3 CUPS**

2 (8-inch) whole-grain pita bread rounds

1 tablespoon extra-virgin olive oil

Kosher salt or coarse sea salt

1. Preheat the oven to 325°F.

2. Using a knife, cut the pita rounds into 1½-inch-thick strips. Turn the strips 90 degrees and cut across the strips, every 1½ inches, so that you end up with 1½-inch squares.

3. Arrange the pita pieces on two baking sheets. Brush the pieces with the olive oil and then sprinkle with salt to taste. Bake until the chips are lightly brown and crisp, 15 to 20 minutes.

4. Let the chips cool completely on the baking sheets. The chips will continue to crisp up as they cool. Pack the chips in a zipper-top plastic bag or other airtight container.

Caraway, Onion, *and* Potato Crackers

The most prominent flavor of this cracker comes from caraway seeds, the fruit of the caraway plant, which comes from Asia, Europe, and Africa. Caraway seeds are commonly used in European cuisine, particularly in savory dishes and liqueurs. You may find the flavor to be similar to rye bread, which also uses the seeds. These crackers keep for 2 weeks. **MAKES ABOUT 12 DOZEN CRACKERS**

1. In a medium-size bowl, combine the flour, baking powder, kosher salt, onion powder, and caraway seeds. Using a fork, work in the potatoes and vegetable oil. Add the water, 1 tablespoon at a time, until the mixture becomes a slightly sticky dough. Wrap the dough in plastic wrap and refrigerate for at least 1 hour.

2. Preheat the oven to 350°F. Divide the dough in half. Return one half of the dough to the refrigerator, and place the other half on a piece of parchment paper. Using a rolling pin, roll the dough as thin as possible. Sprinkle coarse salt on top. Using a sharp knife or pizza cutter, cut the dough into 1-inch squares. Lift the parchment paper and place the paper with the dough on it on a baking sheet. Bake for 15 minutes, turn the heat down to 300°F, and flip the crackers. Continue baking until the crackers are golden and crisp, 20 to 25 minutes longer.

3. When you remove the first batch from the oven, turn the oven temperature back up to 350°F. Repeat the rolling and baking process with the other half of the dough.

4. Cool the crackers completely on the baking sheets. Package the crackers in small cellophane bags or zipper-top plastic bags.

2 cups all-purpose flour

½ teaspoon baking powder

½ teaspoon kosher salt

1 tablespoon onion powder

1 teaspoon caraway seeds

1 cup cooked mashed potatoes

¼ cup vegetable or canola oil

¼ cup water

Coarse salt, for sprinkling

Care Package CPR

Eating limp crackers can be as unpleasant as chewing on a mealy apple. In your note, let your recipient know that if humidity has gotten to them, the crackers can be crisped again in a single layer in a 350°F oven for 5 to 10 minutes.

Dickie's Nuts *and* Bolts

My father-in-law, Dick, is known for his sugary-sweet goodies such as Jell-O-soaked cake, chocolate-peanut popcorn balls, and chocolate-covered Ritz crackers. However, every year, family members have a special request for his savory snack mix. Dick likes to make several variations, but I've adapted his Italian version. Be sure to make extras for your care package because these "nuts and bolts" will disappear quickly. The mix keeps for up to 3 weeks. (If you're wondering why this is called "nuts and bolts," the Cheerios cereal represents the nuts and the stick pretzels are the bolts.) **MAKES ABOUT 3½ CUPS SNACK MIX**

1 cup mini stick pretzels (about 55 pretzels)

1 cup Corn Chex cereal

½ cup Rice Chex cereal

½ cup Cheerios cereal

½ cup Goldfish crackers

2 tablespoons unsalted butter, melted

1 tablespoon Worcestershire sauce

½ teaspoon celery salt

¼ teaspoon garlic powder

¼ teaspoon onion powder

¼ teaspoon dried oregano

¼ teaspoon dried thyme

1. Preheat the oven to 250°F. Grease two baking sheets.

2. In a large bowl, combine the pretzels, cereals, and crackers. In another large bowl, mix the butter, Worcestershire, celery salt, garlic powder, onion powder, oregano, and thyme. Add the cereal mixture and toss to combine. Scatter the mixture onto the baking sheets and bake until it's dry and golden brown, 20 to 25 minutes, stirring every 5 minutes.

3. Allow the snack mixture to cool completely on the pans. Pack the snack mix in zipper-top plastic bags, cellophane bags, or airtight containers.

Golden Cheddar Coins

The winning combination of shortening and butter gives these crackers a flaky texture, buttery flavor, and, most important, longevity. These sturdy crackers will keep for 2 weeks when stored away from humidity. **MAKES 7 TO 8 DOZEN CRACKERS**

1 cup all-purpose flour

¼ teaspoon baking powder

¼ teaspoon freshly ground black pepper

4 tablespoons (½ stick) cold unsalted butter, cut into small pieces

¼ cup vegetable shortening, cut into small pieces

1 large egg

8 ounces grated sharp cheddar cheese

1. In the bowl of a food processor, combine the flour, baking powder, and black pepper. Pulse a few times until well mixed.

2. Add the butter and shortening to the flour mixture and process until it resembles coarse crumbs. Mix in the egg and cheese, and process until the mixture forms a dough, 1 to 2 minutes.

3. Divide the dough into four equal parts and then transfer each part to plastic wrap or waxed paper. Shape the dough into cylinders about 12 inches long and 1½ inches in diameter. Wrap and refrigerate the dough for 2 hours.

4. Preheat the oven to 350°F. Line two baking sheets with parchment paper or silicone baking liners.

5. Slice the dough into ¼-inch-thick slices and place on the prepared baking sheets, 1 inch apart. Bake until the edges of the crackers are slightly brown, 10 to 12 minutes.

6. Cool completely on the baking sheets. Repeat with the remaining dough. Pack the crackers in zipper-top plastic bags and then put the bags in a food-safe tin. Use crumpled parchment or waxed paper to fill empty spaces in the tin.

Chicago-Style Nuts *and* Crackers

A Chicago institution, Garrett's Popcorn has been serving up its blend of cheese and caramel popcorn around the city for decades. While it sounds bizarre, the sharp taste of cheese coupled with the sweet and salty flavors of caramel just seems to work. Inspired by the famous snack, I made a variation using nuts and cheese-flavored crackers. If you can locate orange cheddar cheese powder, give the snack a little dusting to give it an orange hue. This mix keeps well for up to 3 weeks.

MAKES 5 TO 7 CUPS SNACK MIX

1. Line a baking sheet with parchment paper or nonstick foil. Place the nuts in a large bowl.

2. In a small saucepan over medium heat, melt together the butter, brown sugar, corn syrup, and salt. When the mixture begins to bubble, turn off the heat, add the baking soda, and stir to incorporate. Pour the mixture over the nuts and stir to combine. Transfer the nuts to the prepared baking sheet and allow to cool at room temperature.

3. Combine the nuts with the popcorn (if using), the crackers, and the sesame sticks. Pack the snack mix in zipper-top plastic bags or other airtight containers.

2 cups lightly salted mixed nuts, such as walnuts, pecans, cashews, and/or peanuts

2 tablespoons unsalted butter

2 tablespoons packed light brown sugar

2 tablespoons light corn syrup

¼ teaspoon kosher salt

¼ teaspoon baking soda

2 cups cheddar cheese popcorn (optional)

1 cup cheddar cheese–flavored crackers, such as Goldfish or Cheez-Its

1 cup sesame sticks

Black Pepper and Rosemary Crackers

The secret to getting these crackers extra crisp and flaky is to roll the dough as thin as possible. I like rolling the dough out on parchment paper so I don't have to worry about it sticking to my work surface. Once the dough is rolled, you can just lift the parchment and place it on a baking sheet. Make sure your crackers are completely dry before packing them. If stored correctly, they'll keep for more than 1 month. **MAKES 16 TO 17 DOZEN CRACKERS**

1. Preheat the oven to 400°F.

2. In a medium-size bowl, combine the flour, baking powder, pepper, rosemary, and kosher salt. Using a fork, mix the olive oil into the dry ingredients. Drizzle in ¾ cup of the water. Stir until the mixture forms a ball of dough, adding more water if necessary. It should be a little sticky, but not wet. Divide the dough in half. Place one half on a piece of parchment paper and cover the other half with a tea towel to keep it from drying out. Using a rolling pin, roll the dough so that it becomes a very thin sheet, using extra flour if necessary to keep it from sticking. It may take some time to do this, but the thinner you can get the dough, the better.

3. Place the dough and parchment paper on a baking sheet. In a small bowl, mix the egg white with the remaining 2 tablespoons water and brush the mixture over the dough. Sprinkle sea salt over the dough. Using a pizza cutter or a knife, cut the dough into 1-inch squares. Repeat the process with the other half of the dough and place on a second baking sheet.

4. Bake until the crackers are crisp and lightly browned, rotating the sheets halfway through baking, 15 to 18 minutes.

5. Let the crackers cool completely on the pans. They will crisp up more as they cool. Snap the crackers apart, if necessary. Pack the crackers in cellophane bags, zipper-top plastic bags, or airtight containers.

2 cups all-purpose flour, plus more for rolling

1 teaspoon baking powder

1 teaspoon freshly cracked black pepper

1 teaspoon dried rosemary, crumbled

½ teaspoon kosher salt

¼ cup extra-virgin olive oil

¾ cup plus 2 tablespoons water

1 large egg white

Flaky sea salt, for sprinkling

Oven-Baked Potato Crisps

I received my first mandoline slicer more than 10 years ago, when I was reviewing kitchen products for a website. Having never used one before, I was astounded by how quickly and evenly I could slice fruits and vegetables for dishes or snacks. Even after culinary school and stints in professional kitchens, I still use that same mandoline and consider it an indispensable part of my kitchen. You can certainly slice the potatoes for this recipe with a sharp knife, but they may not be as thin or uniform. When using a mandoline, be sure to use a hand guard—it could save you from a kitchen disaster. These crisps will keep for 1 week. **MAKES ABOUT 4 TO 5 CUPS**

2 medium-size russet potatoes, scrubbed

3 tablespoons extra-virgin olive oil

1 teaspoon garlic powder or paprika (optional)

Sea salt or kosher salt

1. Using a mandoline or sharp knife, slice the potatoes into ⅛-inch-thick slices. Soak in cool water to cover for 30 to 60 minutes. (The longer you soak, the crispier your chips will be.)

2. Preheat the oven to 400°F. Place a greased oven-safe metal rack on each of two baking sheets; set aside.

3. Drain the potatoes and place in a single layer on lint-free kitchen towels. Cover the potatoes with another towel and press to remove all the moisture. Transfer the potatoes to a large bowl and toss with the olive oil.

4. Arrange the potatoes in a single layer on the racks on the baking sheets. Sprinkle with seasonings, if desired, and salt to taste. Bake for 30 to 35 minutes, until the potatoes are crisp and light brown in color, turning occasionally and removing them as they are done. (You may need to bake some crisps longer than others. It's important to get them completely crisp.) Repeat with the remaining potatoes.

5. Transfer the crisps to paper towels to drain and cool. Pack the cooled crisps in zipper-top plastic bags. Make sure there is enough insulation around the bags in the care packages so the crisps do not break.

Garlic *and* Dill Seasoned Pretzels

These pretzels are a riff on a brand of delicious seasoned pretzels that I used to gobble down while in boarding school. A friend's mother used to send canisters of the pretzels periodically, and they'd be gone in a matter of days. While these pretzels are not exactly what we had, they come pretty close. Perfect for sending long distances, they'll keep for more than 2 weeks if stored properly—though I doubt they will remain uneaten for that long! **MAKES ABOUT 4 CUPS**

1. Preheat the oven to 250°F. Grease two baking sheets.

2. In a medium-size bowl, mix the Worcestershire, oil, onion powder, dill weed, garlic powder, and cayenne. Add the pretzels and stir to combine thoroughly. Transfer the pretzels to the baking sheets and bake until the pretzels appear dry and the spices adhere to them, 15 to 20 minutes.

3. Let the pretzels cool completely on the baking sheet. Transfer the pretzels to a food-safe tin.

8 teaspoons Worcestershire sauce

4 teaspoons vegetable or canola oil

1 teaspoon onion powder

1 teaspoon dried dill weed

½ teaspoon garlic powder

Pinch of cayenne pepper

4 cups twist or stick pretzels

Sriracha Party Nuts

Some people refer to sriracha as "rooster sauce" because of the stately bird emblazoned on the hot sauce bottles. In recent years, this fiery red sauce with hints of garlic and vinegar has gained a following among chefs, food enthusiasts, and heat seekers. Here I've used it to flavor and deliver a serious punch to ordinary nuts; this mix will keep for 2 to 3 weeks. You can create "party" or "cocktail" care packages and include these along with a bottle opener, a deck of cards, and whatever else you think will spice up an ordinary night at home. **MAKES ABOUT 3 CUPS NUTS**

2 tablespoons sriracha hot sauce

2 teaspoons soy sauce

2 teaspoons vegetable or canola oil

½ teaspoon sugar

1 cup lightly salted peanuts

1 cup roasted almonds

1 cup roasted cashews

1. Preheat the oven to 300°F. Grease two baking sheets.

2. In a medium-size bowl, combine the sriracha, soy sauce, oil, and sugar. Stir until combined. Toss in all of the nuts and stir until completely covered. Spread out the nuts on the baking sheets and bake for 10 to 15 minutes, until the seasonings appear to adhere to the nuts, stirring halfway through.

3. Let the nuts cool on the baking sheet. Pack the nuts in a food-safe tin or Mason jar.

Ridiculously Easy Bagel Chips

Before bagel chips started populating supermarket shelves, bagel stores sold their leftover bagels by slicing them and toasting them in the oven until they were dry and crisp. Next time you have leftover bagels, don't toss them—save them for your next care package. These chips will keep for up to 2 weeks. Jazz them up by sprinkling the rounds with various seasoning combos, if you like: salt and pepper, curry powder, za'atar, and so on. Just be sure to brush or spray a little bit of olive oil on the rounds after baking and before seasoning to ensure that the spices will stick.
MAKES ABOUT 4 CUPS

2 bagels (any flavor you prefer; I like cinnamon-raisin or "everything")

1. Preheat the oven to 375°F.

2. Using a serrated knife, carefully slice the bagels horizontally into ⅛-inch-thick slices, so that you have thin rounds of bagels. Alternatively, you can cut through the bagels vertically for smaller chips.

3. Arrange the slices in a single layer on two baking sheets. Bake until the slices are lightly browned and dry, 10 to 12 minutes (or 8 to 10 minutes if you slice the bagels vertically).

4. Let the bagel chips cool completely on the baking sheets. The chips will get crisper as they cool. Pack the chips in zipper-top plastic bags and make sure they are cushioned in the care package to avoid breakage.

Old Bay Nut Mix

With roots in the Chesapeake Bay area, Old Bay Seasoning is made from a blend of celery salt, paprika, black pepper, and cayenne and is typically used on crabs or other seafood. In this recipe, I toss it in with mixed nuts to create a savory snack that can be served up at parties or with an after-work drink. The mix keeps for 3 weeks. **MAKES ABOUT 2 CUPS NUTS**

1. Preheat the oven to 325°F. Grease a baking sheet.

2. In a medium-size bowl, combine the butter, Worcestershire, Old Bay, hot sauce, and garlic powder. Add the nuts and stir to combine. Transfer to the baking sheet and bake for 20 minutes, stirring halfway through.

3. Allow the nuts to cool completely on the baking sheet. Pack the cooled nuts in a zipper-top plastic bag, Mason jar, or other airtight container.

2 tablespoons unsalted butter, melted

2 tablespoons Worcestershire sauce

2 teaspoons Old Bay Seasoning

1 teaspoon hot sauce of your choice

¾ teaspoon garlic powder

2 cups mixed salted nuts, such as cashews, peanuts, almonds, and/or walnuts

LIGHT
as AIR

While "healthy" foods and snacks sometimes come off as bland, tasteless "diet" foods, these recipes beg to differ. From Rosemary and Olive Oil Popcorn to Oven-Roasted Spiced Chickpeas to Chocolate-Covered Dried Figs, these treats are both packed with flavor and loaded with healthy ingredients that won't weigh anyone down. Throw a few of these treats into a package along with more decadent confections, or put together an altogether healthy care package for your loved one.

Oven-Roasted Spiced Chickpeas

Popular in Indian cooking, chickpeas (also known as garbanzo beans) are an important source of nutrients, such as protein and carbohydrates, as well as fiber. Frequently used in main courses, they are also used in snack mixes. Instead of frying them, I discovered that you can roast them in the oven and still get an irresistibly delicious and crunchy snack. I've coated these chickpeas with a blend of Indian spices, but feel free to experiment with other blends such as curry mixes and garam masala. Once they are baked, they are easy to ship anywhere because of their durability and will keep for 3 weeks. **MAKES ABOUT 2 CUPS CHICKPEAS**

2 (15-ounce) cans chickpeas

1 tablespoon extra-virgin olive oil

½ teaspoon kosher salt

¾ teaspoon ground cumin

¼ teaspoon ground coriander

⅛ teaspoon cayenne pepper

⅛ teaspoon ground turmeric

1. Preheat the oven to 350°F.

2. Drain the chickpeas in a colander and rinse very well under cool running water. Transfer the chickpeas to paper towel–lined baking sheets. Shake the pans several times so the paper towels can absorb the extra water. Use extra paper towels to pat the chickpeas dry, if necessary.

3. In a medium-size bowl, combine the olive oil, salt, and spices. Add the chickpeas and toss so that the spices coat the beans. Spread the chickpeas out on two baking sheets (without paper towels). Roast for 40 to 50 minutes, shaking the trays every 10 to 15 minutes. The chickpeas are done when they are brown and crispy and rattle in the pan when shaken.

4. Let the chickpeas cool on the pans on a rack. Pack the chickpeas in zipper-top plastic bags or glass jars.

Sesame-Kale Chips

As a registered dietitian, I can't say enough about the wonders of kale. Sometimes used as an ornamental vegetable, kale is a superfood that's packed with lots of vitamins and minerals that keep our bodies in tip-top condition. When I first heard about baked kale chips, I thought they were a great idea, but I was deterred by the cost of the packaged kinds sold in health food stores. The great news is that you can make your own for a fraction of the cost. They ship well, too, and keep for up to 10 days. Just make sure that the container they are stored in is well packed so there is no room for shifting. **MAKES ABOUT 10 CUPS**

1. Preheat the oven to 300°F. Line two baking sheets with parchment paper or silicone baking liners; set aside.

2. Wash and dry the kale thoroughly. Using your hands or a knife, remove the kale leaves from the tough and fibrous stalks. Cut or tear the leaves into bite-size pieces.

3. In a medium-size bowl, combine the sesame oil, soy sauce, and sesame seeds. Add the kale and massage the marinade into the leaves. Arrange half of the leaves in a single layer on the prepared baking sheets. Bake until the leaves are dry and crisp, 15 to 20 minutes. Repeat with the remaining leaves.

4. Cool the chips on the baking sheets on a rack. Place the chips in an airtight glass or plastic container, packing enough chips so that there is little room for shifting during shipping.

1 large bunch lacinato or curly kale (about 1½ pounds)

2 tablespoons sesame oil

2 teaspoons reduced-sodium soy sauce

1 teaspoon toasted sesame seeds (see page 153)

Storing Sesame Oil

Light and heat can damage oil and make it become rancid. While it's preferable to store sesame oil in the refrigerator, if you don't have the space, it's fine to store it in a cool, dark place. If the oil ever takes on a bad smell or taste, discard it. As a general buying tip, purchase the smallest bottle you think you need.

Apricot-Almond Granola Bars

Wholesome and energizing, these snack bars are easy to make and extremely portable, and they keep for up to 10 days. Once the bars have cooled, wrap them individually. They are perfect for students, travelers, athletes, or those in the Armed Forces who need high-energy snacks that won't weigh them down. **MAKES 12 BARS**

2 cups old-fashioned rolled oats

1 cup chopped dried apricots

1 cup chopped toasted almonds (see page 95)

Pinch of salt

6 tablespoons vegetable or canola oil

¼ cup honey

¼ cup light corn syrup

¼ cup pure maple syrup

½ teaspoon pure vanilla extract

1. Preheat the oven to 350°F. Line two 5 x 9-inch loaf pans with parchment paper, leaving extra for overhang; set aside.

2. In a medium-size bowl, combine the oats, apricots, almonds, and salt.

3. In a small, heavy-bottomed saucepan over medium heat, combine the oil, honey, corn syrup, and maple syrup. When the mixture comes to a simmer, remove the pan from the heat and stir in the vanilla with a heatproof spatula. Pour the mixture over the oat mixture and stir until the oats are completely coated. Transfer the mixture to the prepared pans and firmly press it into the bottom of the pans. Bake until the edges begin to brown, 20 to 25 minutes.

4. Allow the bars to cool in the pans. While they are still slightly warm, grasp the edges of the parchment paper and pull the bars out of the pans. Cut each loaf crosswise into 6 bars, for a total of 12 bars, and transfer to a rack to cool completely. Wrap the bars individually with waxed or parchment paper or plastic wrap, seal with tape, and pack in a zipper-top plastic bag. Alternatively, layer unwrapped bars in an airtight container, separating the layers with waxed or parchment paper.

Cherry-Vanilla Granola

Sweet and tart, this crunchy treat will go the distance when it comes to shipping, as it's long-lasting (it keeps for 1 month) and won't crumble into bits and pieces. Make a double batch, if you like, and save half for yourself. Pack in Mason jars for a decorative touch in the care package. **MAKES ABOUT 4 CUPS GRANOLA**

1. Preheat the oven to 275°F. Line a baking sheet with parchment paper, foil, or a silicone baking liner; set aside.

2. In a large bowl, combine the oats, coconut, brown sugar, and salt.

3. In a small saucepan over low heat, bring the oil, honey, maple syrup, and water to a simmer. Remove the pan from the heat and stir in the vanilla. Pour the hot syrup over the oat mixture. Stir to combine.

4. Spread the mixture onto the baking sheet and bake until golden brown, 35 to 50 minutes. Check periodically to make sure the granola does not burn. Add the almonds, stir, and bake for 10 minutes longer.

5. Cool the pan on a rack for 20 minutes. Add the dried cherries and stir to combine. Pack the granola in cellophane bags, Mason jars, zipper-top plastic bags, or other airtight containers.

2 cups old-fashioned rolled oats

½ cup sweetened shredded coconut

2 tablespoons packed light brown sugar

¼ teaspoon salt

3 tablespoons vegetable or canola oil

2 tablespoons honey

2 tablespoons pure maple syrup

1 tablespoon water

½ teaspoon pure vanilla extract

½ cup slivered almonds

½ cup dried tart cherries

Chocolate-Covered Dried Figs

Surprise a faraway loved one with this deeply rich and satisfying snack that is actually good for you! High in antioxidants, which can help fight off cell damage, this decadent treat is packed with a lot of flavor, so only a couple of pieces are needed to satisfy a sweet tooth. Layer the figs between waxed paper in a candy box or tin and tie with a festive ribbon. They should keep for 3 weeks or even longer if stored in a cool, dry place. MAKES 40 TO 45 FIGS

12 ounces dried figs (40 to 45 figs)

8 ounces dark chocolate (60% to 70% cacao), melted and tempered (see page 149)

1. Line a baking sheet with waxed or parchment paper.

2. Holding the figs by their stem ends, dunk the bottom halves into the melted chocolate. Set the figs on the prepared baking sheet to dry.

3. When the chocolate has completely set, place the figs in an airtight container, separating the layers with waxed paper.

About Figs

Figs are a highly versatile fruit that can be purchased fresh or dried, eaten raw or cooked, and used in sweet or savory dishes. There are many varieties, but two of the most common are Calimyrna and Black Mission. Calimyrna figs are yellow-green in color and somewhat nutty in flavor; Black Mission figs are deep purple and very sweet. You can find dried versions of both varieties in supermarkets or online. If stored properly, they can last up to two years, making them a great healthy addition to any care package.

TEMPERED CHOCOLATE

You may have heard the term *tempering* on a cooking show or read about it in a food magazine, but what is it? Tempering is a very important technique in candy making that helps chocolate retain its glossy and shiny appearance and gives it a snap when broken into. It's also important because it raises the melting temperature of chocolate so that the finished confection won't melt on contact with your fingers. This is especially important for care packages, since even slight temperature fluctuations can affect the appearance and behavior of chocolate.

There are several ways to temper chocolate, but I find the simplest way is to follow the "seeding" method. In a large heatproof bowl set over a pot of simmering water, melt two-thirds of your dark chocolate chunks or chips and bring the temperature to 115°F (it helps to have a candy thermometer for this). Remove the bowl from the pot of water (being careful not to get any water in the bowl), and begin to vigorously stir the chocolate, gradually adding the remaining chopped chocolate to the bowl. Stop stirring and adding chocolate when the temperature reaches 90°F. Test the chocolate by dipping a spoon into it and spreading the chocolate on a piece of parchment paper. Refrigerate the paper for 2 minutes. If the chocolate is dry to the touch and glossy, and has a slight snap, it is tempered. If not, do not fret. Chocolate can be unpredictable, and tempering takes practice. The good news is that if it doesn't work out the first time, you can use the same chocolate to try again. All you'll need are a few more chocolate chunks or chips to add once your chocolate is back up to temperature.

Antioxidant Berry-Nut Mix

This incredibly nutritious and great-tasting snack mix incorporates ingredients that have high levels of antioxidants, which are thought to help our bodies fight disease and keep our immune systems strong. The mix is great for shipping to loved ones who live far away (the mix will keep for at least 1 month) and who have an interest in health and fitness. **MAKES ABOUT 6 CUPS SNACK MIX**

2 cups dried blueberries

1½ cups walnuts

1 cup semisweet or dark chocolate chips

1 cup dried cherries

½ cup dried cranberries

In a large bowl, combine all of the ingredients. Pack the mixture in zipper-top plastic bags.

Portion It Out

While dried fruit is a healthy snack option, it's still calorically dense and may not be as satisfying as a piece of fresh fruit. Prevent overeating by portioning out the mix into ½-cup bags.

Baked Banana Chips

Unlike store-bought banana chips, which are usually fried and have an artificial taste about them, these chewy chips are the real deal. Concentrated with the real flavor of bananas, these chips are ideal for kids, those who are on the go, and athletes who may need quick energy boosts. Pack them by themselves or mix them with other dried fruits for a healthy snack. Because of their semihard and chewy texture, they are great for care packages and keep for more than 10 days.

MAKES ABOUT 1 CUP BANANA CHIPS

1. Preheat the oven to 225°F. Line two baking sheets with parchment paper or silicone baking liners.

2. Peel the bananas and slice into ¼-inch-thick pieces. Arrange the banana slices in a single layer on the prepared pans. Lightly coat the bananas with cooking spray and bake for 2½ to 3 hours, turning the pieces every 30 minutes. The bananas are done when they are caramelized around the edges and dry yet still pliable.

3. Let the bananas cool in the pans on a rack. Pack the chips in zipper-top plastic bags.

2 medium-size green-yellow bananas (do not use ripe bananas)

Nonstick cooking spray

Rosemary *and* Olive Oil Popcorn

Popcorn is a great addition to care packages. Not only does it weigh very little, it also survives long journeys and keeps well for more than 2 weeks. I gave this popcorn a healthier profile by using heart-healthy olive oil and fresh rosemary. For an extra flavor kick, sprinkle some Parmesan cheese over the popcorn. Be aware that doing so may shorten the shelf life of the popcorn, so if you like, just mention the cheese as a serving suggestion in a note to your recipient. **MAKES ABOUT 8 CUPS POPCORN**

2 tablespoons extra-virgin olive oil

1 sprig fresh rosemary

1 garlic clove, smashed

⅓ cup popcorn kernels

Kosher salt and freshly cracked black pepper

1. In a large pot over low heat, heat the oil. Add the rosemary and garlic and gently infuse the oil for 5 minutes. (You can infuse for longer if you want a stronger flavor.) Remove and discard the rosemary and garlic.

2. Increase the heat to medium-high and add the popcorn kernels to the pot. Cover with a tight-fitting lid. When the kernels begin to pop, shake the pot vigorously until the popping slows down, 2 to 3 minutes. Remove the pot from the heat and season the popcorn with salt and cracked black pepper to taste.

3. Let the popcorn cool completely, then pack in zipper-top plastic bags or other airtight containers.

Everything Crackers

Dry and crisp, these savory snacks will keep for months when stored in an airtight container. Pack them in cellophane or decorative snack bags and seal tightly so that air and moisture cannot get in. When you send them to your loved ones, suggest serving them with cheese, hummus, or a favorite spread.
MAKES ABOUT 7 DOZEN CRACKERS

1. Preheat the oven to 400°F.

2. In a medium-size bowl, combine the flours, baking powder, kosher salt, and garlic powder. Using a fork, mix the oil into the dry ingredients. Drizzle in ¾ cup of the water. Stir until the mixture forms a ball of dough, adding more water if necessary. It should be a little sticky but not wet.

3. Divide the dough in half. Place one half on a piece of parchment paper and cover the other half with a tea towel to keep it from drying out. Using a rolling pin, roll the dough so that it becomes a very thin sheet, using extra flour if necessary to keep it from sticking. It may take some time to do this, but the thinner you can get the dough, the better.

4. Place the dough and parchment paper on a baking sheet. In a small bowl, mix the egg white with the remaining 2 tablespoons water and brush half of the mixture over the dough. Sprinkle half of the sesame seeds, poppy seeds, and flaky salt over the dough. Using a pizza cutter or a knife, cut the dough into 1 x 2-inch rectangles. Repeat the rolling, seasoning, and cutting process with the other half of the dough, placing it on a second baking sheet.

5. Bake for 15 to 18 minutes, until the crackers are crisp and lightly browned, rotating the trays halfway through baking.

6. Let the crackers cool completely on the baking sheets on a rack. They will continue to crisp up as they cool. Pack the crackers in zipper-top plastic bags, cellophane bags, or other airtight containers.

1 cup all-purpose flour, plus more for rolling

1 cup whole-wheat flour

1 teaspoon baking powder

½ teaspoon kosher salt

¼ teaspoon garlic powder

¼ cup vegetable or canola oil

¾ cup plus 2 tablespoons water

1 egg white

1 teaspoon toasted sesame seeds (see below)

½ teaspoon poppy seeds

Flaky sea salt or kosher salt, for sprinkling

Toasting Seeds

To extract the most flavor from sesame seeds, place the seeds in a small skillet over medium heat and toast until golden and fragrant, 3 to 5 minutes.

Crunchy Spiced Apple Crisps

These light, crisp snacks are incredibly easy to make and long lasting (at least 2 weeks), and they make eating fruit fun. I've tested these on a number of people, including some who dislike eating fruit, and they could not believe that the chips did not have any added sugar or oil. **MAKES ABOUT 2 CUPS**

1. Adjust the oven racks to the middle and upper rack positions and preheat the oven to 250°F. Line two baking sheets with parchment paper or silicone baking mats.

2. Using a mandoline or sharp knife, slice the apples into ⅛-inch-thick slices. Transfer the apple slices to a medium-size bowl. Add the lemon juice and pumpkin pie spice and toss until well combined. Arrange the apple slices in a single layer on the prepared baking sheets. Bake for 2 to 3 hours, checking and turning the slices every 30 minutes. They are done when they are lightly brown and dry and still somewhat flexible.

3. Let the chips cool completely on the baking sheets. They will further dry out and become crunchy as they cool. Pack the chips in an airtight container or zipper-top plastic bag.

2 medium-size apples (use your favorites; I like Gala, Braeburn, or Granny Smith)

2 tablespoons freshly squeezed lemon juice

1 teaspoon ground pumpkin pie spice

Chipotle-Lime Pepitas

Translated from Mexican Spanish, *pepita* means "pumpkin seed" and can refer to either the inside kernel of the seed or the whole unhulled seed. Widely popular in Mexico, pepitas can be eaten as a snack or incorporated into dishes such as salads and *mole* sauce. They contain healthy fats, as well as protein, iron, fiber, and zinc. These seasoned pepitas will keep for 1 week. **MAKES ABOUT 1 CUP PEPITAS**

4 teaspoons freshly squeezed lime juice

2 teaspoons vegetable or canola oil

½ teaspoon kosher salt

½ teaspoon chipotle chile powder

1 cup shelled unsalted pepitas

1. Preheat the oven to 250°F. Grease a baking sheet.

2. In a medium-size bowl, combine the lime juice, oil, salt, and chili powder. Add the pepitas and stir until the seeds are coated with the mixture. Scatter the seeds in a single layer on the baking sheet. Bake for 25 minutes, stirring every 5 minutes.

3. Let the seeds cool on the baking sheet on a rack. Pack the seeds in a cellophane or zipper-top plastic bag.

GORP (Good Old Raisins and Peanuts)

In high school, I joined an outdoor adventure club called Search & Rescue, and we'd occasionally have weekend camping trips. I used to look forward to these trips because we could get away for a few days and, most important, eat GORP. The acronym for "Good Old Raisins and Peanuts," GORP was essential to our trips. It energized us for hours on the trail and kept indefinitely in our packs. While there are many variations of this classic, here's one that I particularly like, which has a good mix of protein and carbohydrates. **MAKES ABOUT 6 CUPS SNACK MIX**

Combine all of the ingredients in a large bowl. Pack in snack-size zipper-top plastic bags or in one large airtight container.

1 cup peanut butter–filled pretzel nuggets

1 cup Corn Chex

1 cup Cracklin' Oat Bran

1 cup M&Ms candy

½ cup raisins

½ cup dried cranberries

½ cup lightly salted roasted almonds

½ cup lightly salted peanuts

Tropical Fruit Medley

With a shelf life of more than a month, this portable snack is easy to ship and makes a great and healthy gift for those who long for the tropics. Package the treat in ½-cup portions. **MAKES ABOUT 6 CUPS SNACK MIX**

2 cups unsalted roasted macadamia nuts

1 cup dried mango pieces

1 cup dried banana chips

1 cup unsweetened shredded coconut

½ cup dried papaya or pineapple pieces

½ cup dried kiwi pieces

Combine all of the ingredients in a large bowl. Pack in zipper-top plastic bags or small Mason jars.

Deep Freeze

Nuts, whole-wheat flour, and unsweetened shredded coconut are among the many baking ingredients that can go rancid quickly if not stored properly. They can stay fresh for at least several months if stored in the freezer in a zipper-top plastic bag. Be sure to do a sniff or taste test before using to make sure they are still good.

ASSEMBLE upon ARRIVAL

This chapter includes a few "DIY" recipes for care packages. Let your loved one put his or her own finishing touches on a batch of cupcakes, bake a fresh pan of brownies, or even make a steaming cup of custom hot chocolate with these mix and kit concepts. All you have to do is supply the instructions and ingredients, package everything up, and then ship. It's that easy!

Classic Hot Chocolate *in a* Jar

When the weather gets chilly, why not send a simple hot chocolate mix that's tailor-made for your sweetie? Simply fill small Mason jars with the mix and then ship. All your loved one has to do is add hot water, shake, and sip. No need even for a mug or a spoon! Feel free to add the variation ingredients to the mix or include them in a separate little plastic bag for custom mixing. **MAKES 1 SERVING**

2 tablespoons nonfat milk powder

1 tablespoon natural unsweetened cocoa powder

1½ teaspoons granulated sugar or turbinado sugar

¼ cup mini marshmallows (optional)

1 tablespoon semisweet mini chocolate chips

One Big Jar

As an alternative, you can package the mix in a larger Mason jar for multiple servings. Your recipient would have to provide a mug and spoon, of course. You can fit about 5 servings in a quart-size jar; add a note that indicates that a generous ½ cup mix is needed for each 5- to 6-ounce serving.

1. Combine all of the ingredients in a small (6-ounce) Mason jar. Repeat with as many jars as you'd like to make.

2. Add a note to the package explaining that to serve, add hot water or milk to the jar, leaving about an inch of clearance at the top. Cover and seal the jar, and shake until the ingredients are all dissolved.

Variations

Spicy: Add a generous pinch of pure chile powder (such as ancho or chipotle) or cayenne pepper.

Mexican: Add a generous pinch of ground cinnamon.

Mocha: Add ¼ teaspoon instant espresso powder or coffee granules.

Butterscotch: Instead of chocolate chips, use butterscotch chips.

Peppermint: Add 1 tablespoon crushed peppermint candy or candy canes.

S'mores Kit

Here's a simple s'mores kit you can throw together and send to the kids while they are at sleep-away camp or to friends and family who enjoy camping in the great outdoors. You can scale the recipe up or down to make it in whatever size you prefer, and it will keep indefinitely. And don't forget, National S'mores Day is August 10! **MAKES 6 S'MORES**

Make sure all of the ingredients are well wrapped, either in their original wrappings or with plastic wrap or in suitable containers. Arrange all of the ingredients in a rustic-looking box or basket and then place in a large clear cellophane bag. Tie the bag with a ribbon.

6 whole graham crackers (broken in half to make 12 squares) or 12 large chocolate wafer cookies, gingersnaps, vanilla wafers, or your favorite cookies

6 marshmallows (or see page 102 for Cinnamon Marshmallows)

6 ounces milk or dark chocolate

6 tablespoons peanut butter or chocolate-hazelnut spread (optional)

Care Package CPR

If you are concerned that your homemade marshmallows might be dry on arrival, include a note to your recipient on how to revive them: Put a slice or two of bread in the tin with the marshmallows. The bread will release moisture that the marshmallows will absorb, making them soft again.

Frosted Chocolate-Cinnamon Cupcakes

Celebrate a loved one's special occasion by sending these lightly spiced cupcakes. Take care in wrapping the cupcakes individually in plastic wrap and then packaging the frosting in an airtight container. While the cupcakes are homemade, the frosting is store-bought, with just a little doctoring (shhh!). The cupcakes keep for 5 days; ship them as quickly as you can so your recipient can enjoy them right away.

MAKES 2 DOZEN CUPCAKES

CUPCAKES

- 1⅔ cups all-purpose flour
- ½ cup Dutch-processed cocoa powder, sifted
- ½ teaspoon baking soda
- 1½ teaspoons ground cinnamon
- 12 tablespoons (1½ sticks) unsalted butter, at room temperature
- 1 cup sugar
- ⅓ cup sour cream
- 2 large eggs, at room temperature
- ½ cup strong brewed coffee
- 1½ teaspoons pure vanilla extract

FROSTING

- 2 (16-ounce) containers chocolate frosting
- 2 teaspoons ground cinnamon
- 1 (7-ounce) box Red Hots cinnamon-flavored candies

1. Preheat the oven to 350°F. Line two 12-cup muffin pans with paper liners; set aside.

2. Make the cupcakes: In a medium-size bowl, combine the flour, cocoa, baking soda, and cinnamon.

3. In the bowl of an electric mixer, beat the butter and sugar on medium speed until light and fluffy. Add the sour cream and then the eggs, one at a time, mixing after each addition. Add the brewed coffee and vanilla. Mix for another minute or until the mixture is fully incorporated. Add the flour mixture and mix on low speed until combined. Pour the batter into the prepared muffin cups. Bake until a toothpick inserted into the center of a cupcake comes out clean, 18 to 20 minutes.

4. Let the cupcakes cool in the pan for 10 minutes before transferring to a rack to cool completely. Wrap the cupcakes individually with plastic wrap and pack in an airtight container.

5. For the frosting, combine the frosting and cinnamon in a medium-size bowl and mix with a spatula until the cinnamon is incorporated. Fill a large airtight plastic container with the frosting.

6. Include a note about refrigerating the frosting if not using right away and topping each cupcake with some Red Hot candies, as desired.

You Finish It! Brownies

Does your loved one enjoy baking? Why not make a brownie mix that can be stored indefinitely and baked whenever a brownie craving hits? You can put this care package together in minutes and not even have to turn on your oven! **MAKES 16 BROWNIES**

1. Label two separate zipper-top plastic bags "Mix #1" and "Mix #2." Add the respective ingredients to each bag and seal them.

2. Create a card that says the recipient will need 8 tablespoons (1 stick) unsalted butter and 2 large eggs. Add the following to the card:

> Place the butter and Mix #1 in a medium-size saucepan over medium-low heat. Stir until melted and combined. Remove from the heat. While the mixture is still slightly warm, stir in the eggs. Add Mix #2 and mix until combined.
>
> Pour the batter into an 8-inch square pan and bake in a 350°F oven until a toothpick inserted into the center of the pan comes out mostly clean, 30 to 35 minutes. Let cool on a rack before cutting into squares.

3. Place the mixes and baking instructions in a large Mason jar and then seal. Wrap the jar with cellophane and tie it with a festive ribbon or raffia.

MIX #1

- 4 ounces unsweetened chocolate
- 1¼ cups vanilla sugar (see below)
- ¼ teaspoon salt

MIX #2

- 1 cup all-purpose flour
- 2 tablespoons natural unsweetened cocoa powder
- ¼ cup toasted walnuts (optional; see page 95)

Vanilla Sugar

Vanilla sugar is simply sugar that's been flavored with vanilla beans or vanilla extract. You can buy it in gourmet shops, but it's much more economical to make your own. Simply cut a vanilla bean pod in half and bury it in a cup of sugar. Store indefinitely to let the vanilla flavor penetrate the sugar.

Nutmeg Butter Cookies with Caramel Spread

Send these to a young person who's away at college for a sweet, fragrant treat that will remind them of their childhood kitchen. These golden, buttery cookies paired with warm caramel make for a decadent treat that's reminiscent of a Twix candy bar, but without the chocolate. There's no need to fuss with a homemade caramel sauce. All the recipient needs to do is microwave the caramels. These cookies will keep for up to 2 weeks. **MAKES ABOUT 8 DOZEN COOKIES**

2¼ cups all-purpose flour

½ teaspoon ground nutmeg

¼ teaspoon salt

1 cup (2 sticks) unsalted butter, at room temperature

⅔ cup sugar

1 large egg, at room temperature

1 teaspoon pure vanilla extract

1 (9.5-ounce) bag caramels

1. In a medium-size bowl, combine the flour, nutmeg, and salt.

2. In the bowl of an electric mixer, beat the butter and sugar on medium speed until light and fluffy. Add the egg and vanilla; mix again until blended. Add the flour mixture and mix on low speed until combined. Divide the dough in half and transfer to two sheets of waxed or parchment paper. Shape the dough into two logs, each 12 to 14 inches in length and 1½ inches in diameter. Wrap the logs in the paper and refrigerate for 2 hours.

3. Preheat the oven to 350°F. Line two baking sheets with parchment paper or silicone baking liners; set aside.

4. Remove the paper from the dough and slice the logs into ¼-inch-thick pieces. Place the cookies on the prepared baking sheets, 1 inch apart. Bake until the edges of the cookies are golden, 10 to 12 minutes.

5. Let the cookies cool on the pans for 5 minutes before transferring them to a rack to cool completely. Pack in zipper-top plastic bags, pressing out any air, or in airtight containers, separating the layers with waxed or parchment paper.

6. Unwrap the caramels and place in a quart-size Mason jar (or two pint-size jars). Seal the jars and attach directions for melting the caramels:

Place the caramels in a microwave-safe glass bowl. Add 1 to 2 teaspoons water. Microwave in 15-second increments until the caramels are melted. Carefully remove the bowl from the oven with a towel or pot holder (it will be extremely hot) and stir the caramel with a heatproof spoon or knife. Continue to microwave in 10-second increments if the caramel is not completely melted. Spread on the cookies.

Note: Do not microwave the caramels in the Mason jar, as the glass may crack.

What's Nutmeg?

Nutmeg comes from the seed of a tropical tree native to Southeast Asia. It's covered by a lacy net that is removed and dried to produce the spice mace. You can find whole nutmeg seeds in most super-markets and grind it yourself on a rasp or grater. Freshly ground is much more intense in flavor than the pre-ground kind, but if you can't find the whole seed, then use ground nutmeg.

MEASUREMENT EQUIVALENTS

Please note that all conversions are approximate.

LIQUID CONVERSIONS

U.S.	Metric
1 tsp	5 ml
1 tbs	15 ml
2 tbs	30 ml
3 tbs	45 ml
¼ cup	60 ml
⅓ cup	75 ml
⅓ cup + 1 tbs	90 ml
⅓ cup + 2 tbs	100 ml
½ cup	120 ml
⅔ cup	150 ml
¾ cup	180 ml
¾ cup + 2 tbs	200 ml
1 cup	240 ml
1 cup + 2 tbs	275 ml
1¼ cups	300 ml
1⅓ cups	325 ml
1½ cups	350 ml
1¾ cups	375 ml
1¾ cups	400 ml
1¾ cups + 2 tbs	450 ml
2 cups (1 pint)	475 ml
2½ cups	600 ml
3 cups	720 ml
4 cups (1 quart)	945 ml
	(1,000 ml is 1 liter)

WEIGHT CONVERSIONS

U.S./U.K.	Metric
½ oz	14 g
1 oz	28 g
1½ oz	43 g
2 oz	57 g
2½ oz	71 g
3 oz	85 g
3½ oz	100 g
4 oz	113 g
5 oz	142 g
6 oz	170 g
7 oz	200 g
8 oz	227 g
9 oz	255 g
10 oz	284 g
11 oz	312 g
12 oz	340 g
13 oz	368 g
14 oz	400 g
15 oz	425 g
1 lb	454 g

OVEN TEMPERATURE CONVERSIONS

°F	Gas Mark	°C
250	½	120
275	1	140
300	2	150
325	3	165
350	4	180
375	5	190
400	6	200
425	7	220
450	8	230
475	9	240
500	10	260
550	Broil	290

RESOURCE GUIDE

INSIDE THE BOX

The following are great sources for note cards, stationery, gift labels, gift wrap and other decorative papers, rubber stamps, decorating pens, embossers, and more.

Crane & Co.
www.crane.com
(800) 268-2281

Kate's Paperie
www.katespaperie.com
(212) 941-9816
(800) 809-9880

Muji
www.muji.us

Paper Source
www.paper-source.com
(888) PAPER-11 (727-3711)

Papyrus
www.papyrusonline.com
(800) 789-1649

Vigo Cards
www.vigocards.com
(212) 532-9122

PACKAGING SUPPLIES

Look to these sources for paper and aluminum baking pans, cellophane bags, decorative boxes in all shapes and sizes, ribbons, and much more.

Amazon
www.amazon.com

Creative Gift Packaging
www.creativegiftpackaging.com
(866) 443-8706

Kitchen Krafts
www.kitchenkrafts.com
(800) 776-0575

N.Y. Cake
www.nycake.com
(800) 942-2539

Party City
www.partycity.com
(800) 727-8924

Wilton
www.wilton.com
(888) 373-4588

PACKING AND SHIPPING SUPPLIES

These are all good sources for shipping supplies such as corrugated mailing boxes, tape, and other packing materials. You can also find inside-of-the-box decorative packing materials at most of these sources. Additionally, most Staples, Office Depot, and OfficeMax stores offer packing and shipping services.

The Container Store
www.containerstore.com
(888) CONTAIN (266-8246)

Michaels
www.michaels.com
(800) MICHAELS (642-4235)

Office Depot
www.officedepot.com
(800) GODEPOT (463-3768)

OfficeMax
www.officemax.com
(800) 283-7674

Paper Mart
www.papermart.com
(800) 745-8800

Staples
www.staples.com
(800) 333-3330

Target
www.target.com
(800) 440-0680

Uline
www.uline.com
(800) 958-5463

SHIPPING

DHL Express
www.dhl-usa.com
(800) CALL-DHL (225-5345)

FedEx
www.fedex.com
(800) GOFEDEX (463-3339)

United Parcel Service (UPS)
www.ups.com
(800) PICK-UPS (742-5877)

United States Postal Service (USPS)
www.usps.com
(800) ASK-USPS (275-8777)

INDEX

Note: Page references in *italics* indicate photographs.

ABOUT THE AUTHOR

Shirley Fan spent six years at the Food Network, where she worked on the network's television shows and its cookbooks. She also helped launch *Food Network Magazine* and was a content producer for FoodNetwork.com. She has written for RealSimple.com and iVillage as well as *Food Network Magazine*. A registered dietitian, Fan graduated from Wesleyan University and has a culinary arts diploma from the Institute of Culinary Education in New York. While in culinary school she was the recipient of a James Beard Foundation Scholarship. She now lives in Chicago with her husband and son. *The Flying Brownie* is her first cookbook.